FUTURE LITERACY WORKBOOK

with AUDIO CD

Sarah Lynn

Future Literacy Workbook with Audio CD

Pearson Education, 10 Bank Street, White Plains, NY 10606 USA

Staff credits: The people who made up the *Literacy Workbook* team, representing editorial, production, design, manufacturing, and marketing are Rhea Banker, Maretta Callahan, Dave Dickey, Gina DiLillo, Christine Edmonds, Oliva Fernandez, Nancy Flaggman, Irene Frankel, and Patricia Wosczyk.

Text composition: S4Carlisle Publishing Services
Text font: 10.5 pt Frutiger PEDG

Illustration credits: Steve Attoe, Kenneth Batelman, Luis Briseno, Laurie Conley, Deborah Crowle, Len Ebert, Scott Fray, Peter Grau, Brian Hughes, Stephen Hutchings, Paul McCusker, Chris Murphy, Roberto Sadi, Steve Schulman, Neli Stewart/NSV Productions, Meryl Treatner, Anna Veltfort.
Photo credits: Cover (top left) Chris Schmidt/iStockphoto.com, (top right) Shutterstock.com, (bottom left) PNC/Getty Images, (bottom right) Chris Schmidt/iStockphoto.com; Page 2 (top) Shutterstock.com, (bottom) David Mager/Pearson; p. 7 (1–5) Shutterstock.com, (6) David Mager/Pearson; p. 9 (1) Shutterstock.com, (2–3) David Mager/Pearson, (4) Shutterstock.com, (5) David Mager/Pearson, (6) Shutterstock.com; p. 14 (1) Dreamstime.com, (2) Stockbyte/Getty Images, (3) Pearson, (4–9) Shutterstock.com; p. 21 (1–3) David Mager/Pearson, (4) Bigstock.com, (5) Shutterstock.com, (6) David Mager/Pearson; p. 22 David Mager/Pearson; p. 38 (1–2) Shutterstock.com, (3–4) David Mager/Pearson, (5–6) Shutterstock.com; p. 39 (1) David Mager/ Pearson, (2–3) Shutterstock.com, (4) David Mager/Pearson, (5) Shutterstock.com, (6) iStockphoto.com; p. 41 Shutterstock.com; p. 47 Shutterstock.com; p. 50 David Mager/Pearson; p. 52 (1) Can Stock Photo Inc., (2–3) Shutterstock.com, (4) Can Stock Photo Inc., (5–6) Shutterstock.com; p. 62 (1–2) Shutterstock.com, (3) iStockphoto.com, (4–9) Shutterstock.com; p. 66 (all) Shutterstock.com; p. 71 (all) Shutterstock.com; p. 78 (1) Photos.com, (2–6) Shutterstock.com, (7) iStockphoto.com, (8) Photos.com, (9) Shutterstock.com; p. 79 (top) Shutterstock.com, (bottom) Shutterstock.com; p. 94 (left to right) David Mager/Pearson, Shutterstock.com, David Mager/Pearson, Dorling Kindersley; p. 95 (top left) Photos.com, (top middle) Can Stock Photo Inc., (top right) Shutterstock.com, (bottom left) Shutterstock.com, (bottom right) Shutterstock.com; p. 98 (1) Shutterstock.com, (2) iStockphoto.com, (3) Sami Sarkis Lifestyles/Alamy, (4) Dreamstime.com, (5–6) Shutterstock.com, (7) Diane Macdonald/Getty Images, (8) Shutterstock.com; p. 99 David Mager/Pearson; p. 102 (1) Rubberball/Alamy, (2–4) Shutterstock.com, (5) Jupiter Images/Comstock/Alamy, (6) Shutterstock.com, (7) I love images/Jupiterimages, (8) iStockphoto.com; p. 110 (1) Jeff Greenberg/ The Image Works, (2) David R. Frazier/PhotoEdit, (3) Rob Crandall/The Image Works, (4) Jeff Greenberg/PhotoEdit, (5) MedioImages/age fotostock, (6) Photodisc/Getty Images, (7) Will & Deni McIntyre/Photo Researchers, Inc., (8) Shutterstock .com; p. 112 (1) David R. Frazier/PhotoEdit (2) Andre Jenny/Alamy, (3) Shutterstock.com, (4) Pixtal/SuperStock, (5) Tom Prettyman/PhotoEdit, (6) David R. Frazier/PhotoEdit, (7) Shutterstock.com, (8) Jeff Greenberg/PhotoEdit; p. 118 (1) Steve Hamblin/ Alamy, (2) Steve Hamblin/Alamy; p. 119 (all) Shutterstock.com; p. 134 (1) MedioImages/Getty Images, (2) Jeff Greenberg/ PhotoEdit, (3) Shutterstock.com, (4) BananaStock/age fotostock, (5) Jeff Greenberg/PhotoEdit, (6) David De Lossy/Getty Images, (7) Frank Herholdt/Getty Images, (8) Kayte M. Deioma/PhotoEdit; p. 136 (1) Dynamic Graphics/Jupiterimages, (2) Michael Newman/PhotoEdit, (3) Shutterstock.com, (4) iStockphoto.com, (5) Dennis MacDonald/PhotoEdit, (6) Shutterstock.com, (7) Jeff Greenberg/PhotoEdit, (8) Dreamstime.com.

ISBN-13: 978-0-13-268020-2
ISBN-10: 0-13-268020-3

Printed in the United States of America
1 2 3 4 5 6 7 8 9 10—V042—16 15 14 13 12

Contents

To the Teacher

Overview

The *Future Literacy Workbook* can be used as a companion to the *Future* Intro Level Student Book, *Future* Student Book 1, or with any beginning-level course where students are **learning to read and write**. It was designed for learners who

- may have limited reading and writing skills in their native language.
- use a non-roman alphabet in their native language.
- need a limited amount of text on each page.
- need simplified practice activities.
- benefit from intensive practice of key words.

Using the *Literacy Workbook*

In a literacy class, the teacher can use the *Future* Intro Level Student Book in class and assign material from the *Literacy Workbook* for homework. The *Literacy Workbook* can also be used as a core text in a low-level literacy classroom because of the unique exercise types and accompanying audio CD.

In a multi-level class, teachers can use the *Future* Intro Level Student Book as a class text and then assign the *Future* Intro Workbook and the *Literacy Workbook*, according to students' needs because the two workbooks correspond in content and page numbers.

The *Literacy Workbook* Approach

Two challenges that literacy learners face are understanding and connecting spoken language to print. The *Literacy Workbook* **establishes meaning first**. Key words are introduced and supported by pictures and audio to help students recognize the meaning of the printed words. Students then **focus on the sounds and letters** of the words. As a final step, students **write the words in meaningful contexts** demonstrating they both understand the words and can write them in print.

Adult literacy learners need multiple avenues to reach their goal of reading and writing in English. The *Literacy Workbook* **offers a multi-sensory approach** by including:

- Visual learning: Students see text and pictures.
- Aural/oral learning: Students listen carefully to spoken English and then practice the pronunciation of sounds, words, and sentences.
- Kinesthetic learning: Students repetitively write letters, words, and sentences to develop their muscle memory of how to write.

Recent studies show that literacy learners have challenges learning grammar. For this reason the *Literacy Workbook* **presents grammar in meaningful chunks** and then **provides guided practice** so that students understand what they are saying and produce the grammar correctly.

The *Literacy Workbook* offers the following:

- **Handwriting practice** on page vii provides letter formation practice for lower case and capital letters. You can use this page along with the **online Worksheets** available at www.futureenglishforresults.com/literacy. These **online Worksheets** show students how to write each letter with the correct sequence of strokes. They also provide extensive practice in writing each letter and writing the alphabet in the correct order. These worksheets can provide extra support for students who already write in a non-roman alphabet or students with poor letter formation. The worksheets can be used independently or in class.

- An **Audio CD** in the back of the book helps learners connect the sounds of English to the printed word. Make sure students know how to operate an audio CD player so they can practice listening outside of the class.
- An **Answer Key** is available online. Go to www.futureenglishforresults.com/literacy. You may want to print several copies so students can use them to work in groups to correct their work. Or you may want to print a copy for each student.
- **Word lists** are available online at www.futureenglishforresults.com/literacy. The lists contain all the words students learn to read and write in each lesson. You can print out the lists for students' independent study. You can use the lists to recycle and review the vocabulary as students work through the *Literacy Workbook.*

Expanding on Exercises in the *Literacy Workbook*

Trace.

- Before students begin tracing, the class practices *skywriting* in unison. Everyone stands up and puts their writing hand and arm out straight. Lead the class, with your back to the class, and draw each letter in the air with a stiff arm. Students follow along as they say each letter aloud. These large arm movements can help learners remember the sequence of strokes in forming each letter.

Write.

- Before students do the activity, ask them to say what they see in the pictures.
- After students complete the exercise and check their answers, they can "say and point" in pairs. In this activity one student reads a word to a partner. The partner listens and points to the correct word. Then they switch roles. For more challenging practice, students can cover the pictures and look only at the word boxes.

Listen. Check your answers.

- After checking their answers, students listen again and repeat each word as they read along.

Cover and write.

- Before students write, read each word aloud so students hear the correct pronunciation. Invite students to ask you to repeat any word. Students say the number of the word they want to hear. Request the repetition of any word by identifying the number of the item in the list.
- After completing the exercise, students evaluate the quality of their handwriting by circling the word on each line that shows their best handwriting.
- To provide more practice, dictate the words for students to write on a separate piece of paper. Students can compare their spelling in pairs, or check against correct spelling on the board.

Listen and circle.

- For a multi-sensory approach, the class, as a group, reads the words aloud before you play the audio.
- After students complete the activity and check their answers, they take turns reading a word to a partner. The partner listens and points to the corresponding word.
- If you would like to offer more writing practice, students close their books and use the audio for a dictation. To provide visual support, draw a short line on the board for each letter in the word. Stop the audio after each word and write it on the board, so students can immediately check their spelling.

Listen and write.

- After students do the exercise, offer multiple opportunities to read the text again and again. First, students read the text silently with pencils down. Next, play the audio—item by item—as students listen and write the missing word. Then students listen to the full audio as they read along silently. As a final fluency practice, students read the story aloud in pairs.

Copy the *Yes* sentences.

- After students complete the activity, they read their *Yes* sentences aloud to a partner.
- Students practice handwriting by copying their *Yes* sentences several times on separate pieces of paper. They can choose the group of sentences they think represent their best handwriting to hand in.
- Finally, students hang their best writing on the classroom wall.

Handwriting Practice

The **handwriting practice** on page vii provides students with letter formation guidelines for capital and lower case letters. You can use this worksheet at the beginning of the semester. Ask students to trace the letters on the handwriting practice page. If a student struggles with any part of the practice, you can offer additional individual practice on letter formation using the online Worksheets available at www.futureenglishforresults.com/literacy.

Handwriting Practice

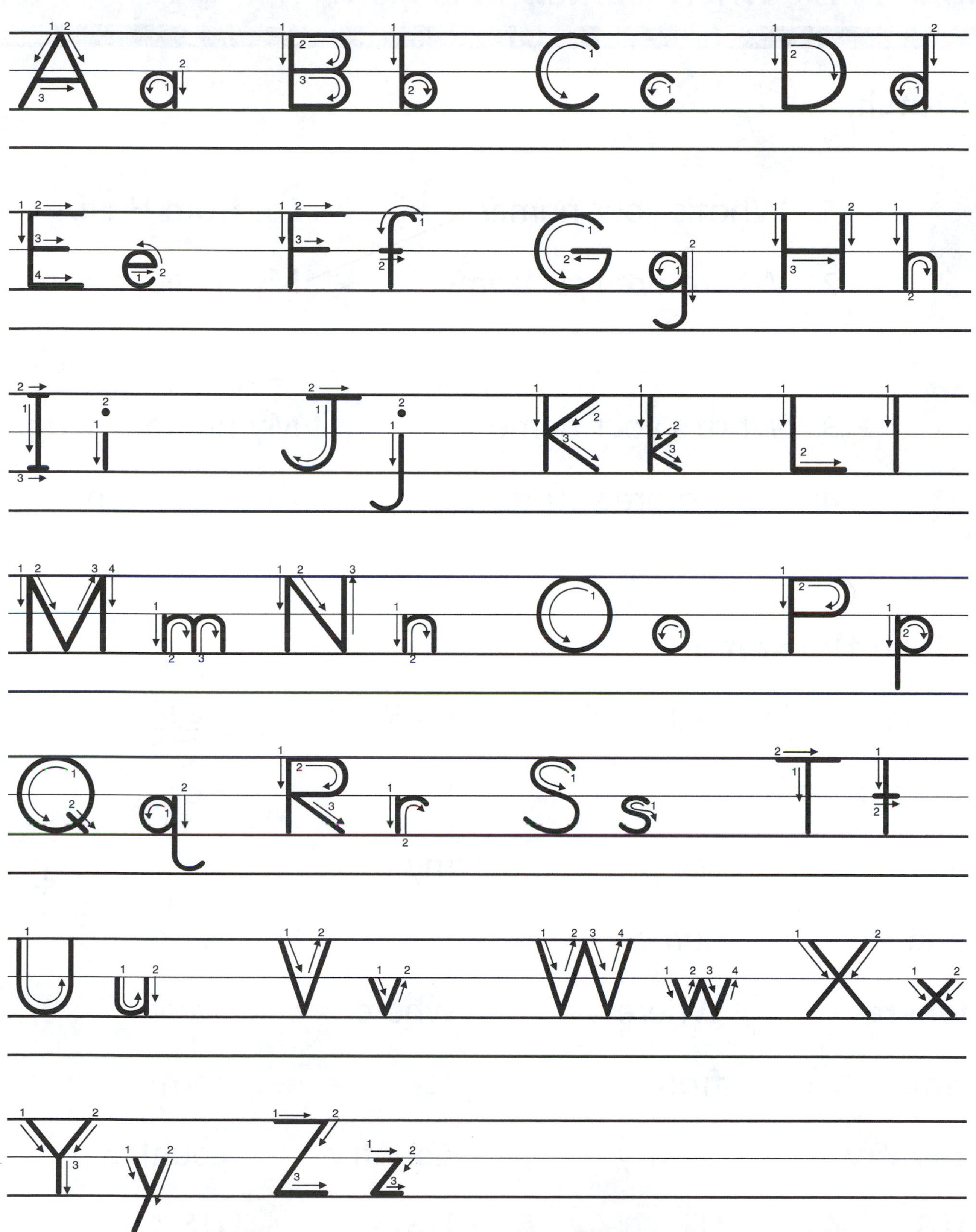

Unit 1: Nice to meet you.

Lesson 1: Ask where someone is from

A Match.

1.	What's your name?	I'm from Haiti.
2.	Where are you from?	My name is Rosa.

3.	What's your name?	My name is Teng.
4.	Where are you from?	I'm from China.

B Circle the same.

1.	**Hello**	hello	help	Hello
2.	**Hi**	hi	Hi	He
3.	**my**	My	my	me
4.	**name**	name	names	Name
5.	**where**	Where	where	were
6.	**from**	from	for	form
7.	**country**	county	Country	country
8.	**U.S.**	US	U.S.	U.S.A.

C T2 Listen and write.

Hello	~~Hi~~	name

A: Hi. My ____________ is Chen.

B: ____________. I'm Pam.

D T3 Listen and write.

from	Where

A: ____________ are you from?

B: I'm ____________ the U.S.

E Write about you. Copy.

My name is ____________. ____________________________

I'm from ____________. ____________________________

Lesson 2: The alphabet

A T4 **Listen. Point to the letters.**

Aa	Bb	Cc	Dd	Ee	Ff	Gg
Hh	Ii	Jj	Kk	Ll	Mm	Nn
Oo	Pp	Qq	Rr	Ss	Tt	
Uu	Vv	Ww	Xx	Yy	Zz	

B **Write. Use capital letters.**

A	B	____	D	____	F	____
H	____	J	____	L	____	N
____	P	____	R	____	T	
____	V	____	X	____	Z	

C **Write. Use lowercase letters.**

a	b	____	d	____	f	____
h	____	j	____	l	____	n
____	p	____	r	____	t	
____	v	____	x	____	z	

Lesson 3: Numbers

A Trace. Copy. Cover and write.

	Trace.	Copy.	Cover and write.
	0	___	___
•	1	___	___
••	2	___	___
•••	3	___	___
••••	4	___	___
•••••	5	___	___
••••••	6	___	___
•••••••	7	___	___
••••••••	8	___	___
•••••••••	9	___	___

B T5 Listen and write.

1. 7 5 4 - 5 5 5 - 3 9 2 1
2. ___ ___ ___ - 5 5 5 - ___ ___ ___ ___
3. ___ ___ ___ - 5 5 5 - ___ ___ ___ ___
4. ___ ___ ___ - 5 5 5 - ___ ___ ___ ___

Lesson 4: *I am, you are*

A Write.

am are

1. I ___am___ a student.
2. You ___are___ a teacher.
3. You ________ my classmate.
4. I ________ in the classroom.
5. You ________ in the library.

B Circle the contractions.

1. You are (You're)
2. I'm I am
3. You're You are
4. I am I'm

C Write the sentences. Use contractions.

1. You are a teacher. ___You're a teacher.___
2. You are from the U.S. ________
3. I am in class. ________

Lesson 5: Introduce someone; *He is, she is*

A Write.

He	She

1. ____She____ is my classmate.

2. ________ is a teacher.

3. ________ is a student.

4. ________ is my friend.

5. ________ is from the U.S.

6. ________ is a teacher.

B Circle the contractions.

1. He is — He's
2. She's — She is
3. He's — He is
4. She is — She's

C T6 Listen and circle.

1. She's — He's
2. She's — He's
3. She's — He's
4. She's — He's
5. She's — He's

D Write the sentences. Use contractions.

1. He is my friend. He's my friend.
2. She is my teacher. ______________________
3. He is a student. ______________________
4. She is a classmate. ______________________
5. He is a teacher. ______________________

Lesson 6: *You're, We're, They're*

A Write.

He's	She's	They're

1. They're students.
2. ____________ a teacher.
3. ____________ a friend.
4. ____________ from the United States.
5. ____________ my classmate.
6. ____________ classmates.

B Circle the contractions.

1. We are We're
2. They're They are
3. You are You're
4. We're We are

C T7 Listen and circle.

1. They're We're You're
2. They're We're You're
3. They're We're You're
4. They're We're You're
5. They're We're You're
6. They're We're You're

D Write the sentences. Use contractions.

1. They are classmates. They're classmates.
2. We are students. ______________________
3. You are from the U.S. ______________________
4. They are my friends. ______________________
5. We are in class. ______________________

Lesson 7: Fill out a form

A Write.

1. My first name is ______________________________.
2. My middle name is ______________________________.
3. My last name is ______________________________.
4. My phone number is ______________________________.
5. I am from ______________________________.

B Write about you.

Adult Education Center

Name ______________________________

First Middle Last

Telephone ____________ – ______________________

Area Code Phone Number

Place of Birth ______________________________

Country

Lesson 8: Ivan's story

A Match.

Students say hello and bow.

Students say hello and kiss.

Students say hello and shake hands.

Students say hello and hug.

B T8 Listen. Check your answers.

C Circle *Yes* or *No* about you.

I hug my classmates.	Yes	No
I shake hands with my classmates.	Yes	No
I bow to my classmates.	Yes	No

Phonics

A T9 **Listen and write.** **Copy.**

m n

1. __ame ____________________
2. __umber ____________________
3. __y ____________________
4. __iddle name ____________________
5. __ew ____________________
6. __eet ____________________

B T10 **Listen and write.** **Copy.**

f h

1. __ello ____________________
2. __riend ____________________
3. __irst name ____________________
4. __i ____________________
5. __rom ____________________
6. __ug ____________________

Unit 2: Welcome to class!

Lesson 1: The classroom

A T11 **Listen and point.**

B **Trace. Copy.**

1 book

2 notebook

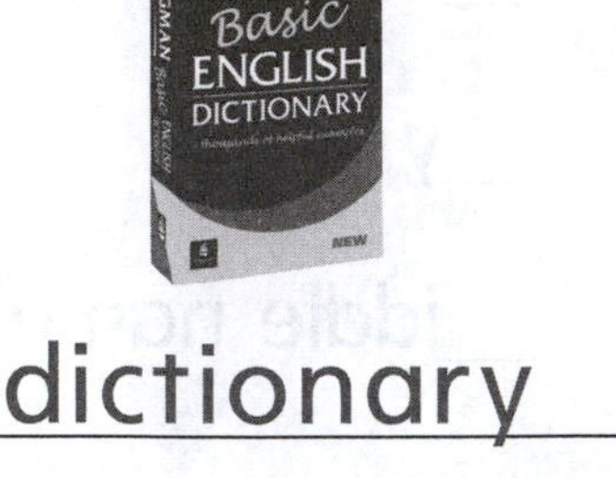

3 dictionary

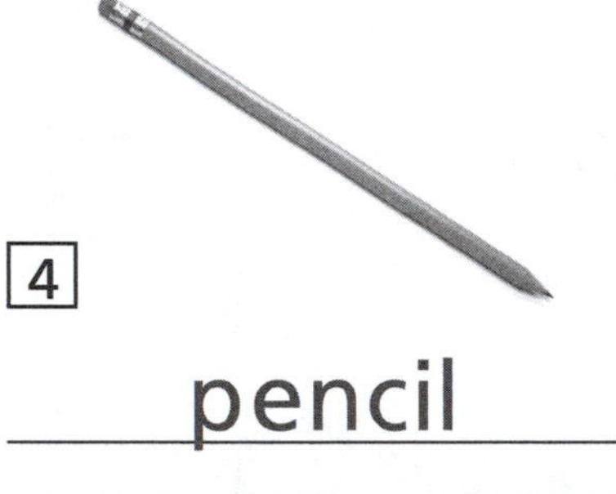

4 pencil

5 pen

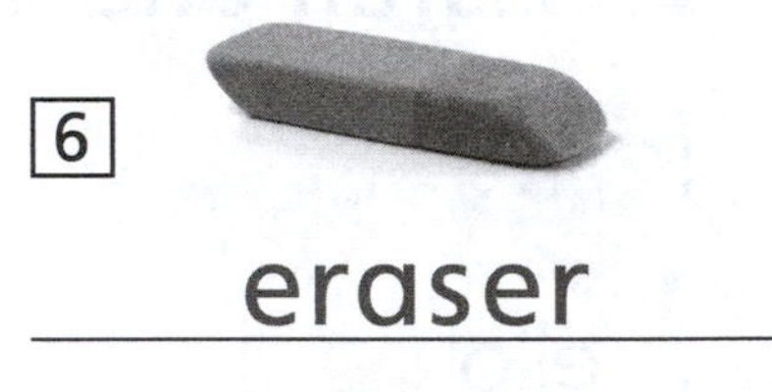

6 eraser

7 paper

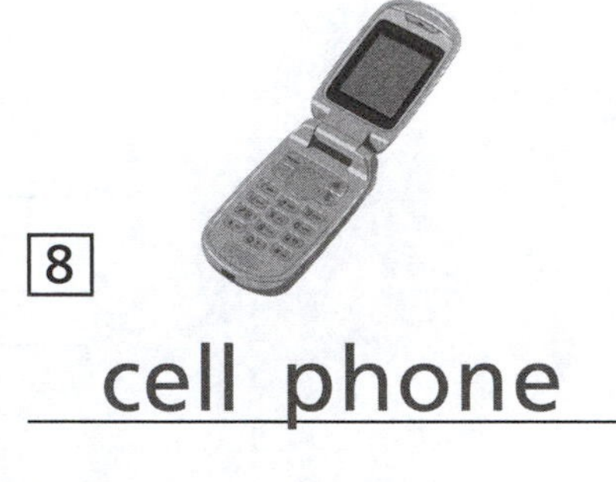

8 cell phone

9 backpack

C Look and circle.

1.	Do you have a pencil?	(Yes, I do.)	No, I don't.
2.	Do you have a backpack?	Yes, I do.	No, I don't.
3.	Do you have a pen?	Yes, I do.	No, I don't.
4.	Do you have a notebook?	Yes, I do.	No, I don't.
5.	Do you have an eraser?	Yes, I do.	No, I don't.

D Write about you.

Yes, I do.	No, I don't.

1. Do you have a book? Yes, I do.
2. Do you have an eraser? ________
3. Do you have a pen? ________
4. Do you have a notebook? ________
5. Do you have a cell phone? ________

Lesson 2: Classroom instructions

A Write.

Turn off
Turn on

Turn on the light.

__________ the light.

Close
Open

__________ your book.

__________ your dictionary.

Put away
Take out

__________ your pencil.

__________ your book.

B  **Listen. Check your answers.**

T12

C T13 Listen and circle.

1. Open (Close)
2. Turn on Turn off
3. Put away Take out
4. Open Don't open
5. Take out Don't take out
6. Turn off Don't turn off

D Write sentences. Use a capital and a period.

1. open your book Open your book.
2. take out your pencil ______
3. close your notebook ______
4. put away your pen ______
5. turn off your cell phone ______
6. don't turn on the light ______

Lesson 3: School

A T14 **Listen and point.**

B **Trace. Copy.**

1 classroom

2 cafeteria

3 library

4 men's room

5 women's room

6 computer lab

7 office

8 bookstore

9 testing room

C Underline the same.

1. **class** classroom classmate
2. **room** classroom women's room men's room
3. **book** notebook bookstore
4. **phone** telephone cell phone

D T15 Listen and write.

book	class	phone	room

1. classroom
2. ________store
3. ________mate
4. cell ________
5. note________
6. men's ________
7. tele________
8. women's ________

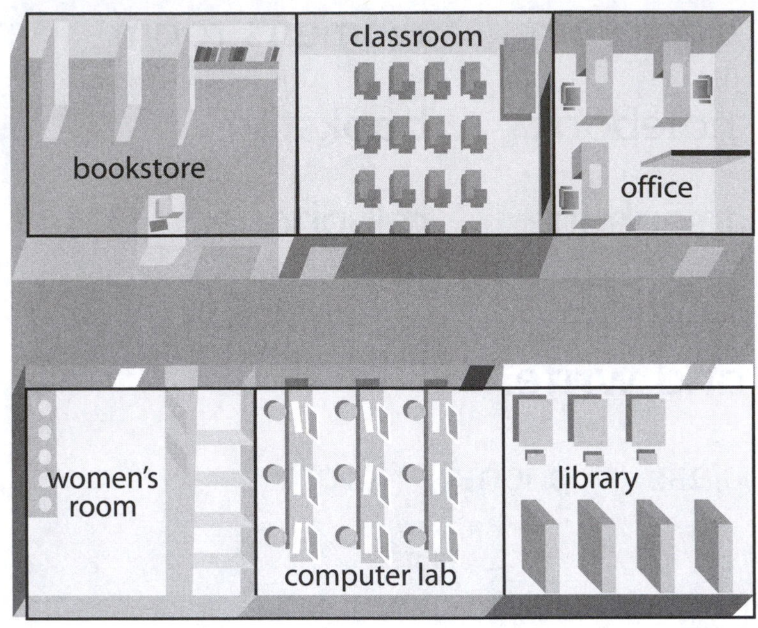

Ⓐ Look. Write.

1. Where is the classroom? Next to the office
2. Where is the office? Across from the ____________
3. Where is the bookstore? Next to the ____________
4. Where is the library? Next to the ____________
5. Where is the women's room? Across from the ____________
6. Where is the computer lab? Across from the ____________

Lesson 5: Fill out a form

A Write.

male female	 1 male	 2 ______
married single	 3 Miss Chan ______	 4 Mrs. Brown ______
Ms. Mr.	 5 ______	 6 ______

B Fill out the form. Write about you.

Vista Learning Center

☐ Mr.
☐ Mrs.
☐ Miss
☐ Ms.

____
Last Name First Name

____
Place of Birth

☐ Male ☐ Married
☐ Female ☐ Single

A Trace.

go to class

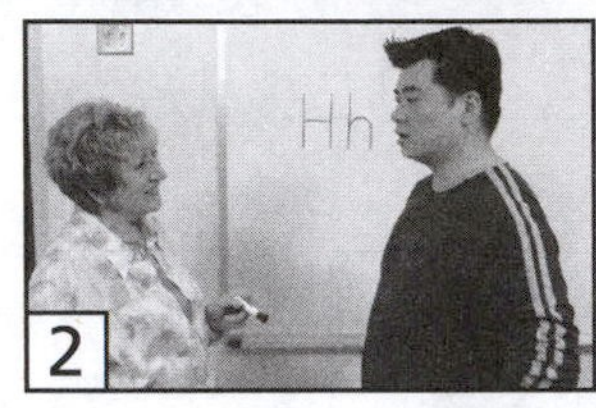

ask questions

use a dictionary

write in my notebook

read signs

practice English

B T16 Listen and write.

ask	go	practice

1. I ________________ to class.
2. I ________________ English with my classmates.
3. I ________________ the teacher questions.

read	use	write

4. I ________________ a dictionary.
5. I ________________ in my notebook.
6. I ________________ signs.

C Circle *Yes* or *No* about you.

I go to class.	Yes	No
I ask questions.	Yes	No
I use a dictionary.	Yes	No
I write in my notebook.	Yes	No
I read signs.	Yes	No

D Copy your *Yes* sentences in your notebook.

A Match.

Students talk in groups.

Students don't talk in class.

Students ask questions.

Students listen to the teacher.

B T17 Listen. Check your answers.

C Circle *Yes* or *No* about your class.

Students talk in groups.	Yes	No
Students talk in class.	Yes	No
Students ask questions.	Yes	No

Phonics

A T18 **Listen and write.** **Copy.**

b p

1. __en ______________________
2. __aper ______________________
3. __ook ______________________
4. __ackpack ______________________
5. __encil ______________________
6. __ut away ______________________

B T19 **Listen and write.** **Copy.**

m n

1. __otebook ______________________
2. __en ______________________
3. __ale ______________________
4. __ext to ______________________
5. __y ______________________

Unit 3: On Time

Lesson 1: Times

A T20 **Listen and point.**

B **Copy.**

0	1	2	3	4	5	6	7	8	9
0	*1*								
10	11	12	13	14	15	16	17	18	19
20	21	22	23	24	25	26	27	28	29
30	31	32	33	34	35	36	37	38	39
40	41	42	43	44	45	46	47	48	49
50	51	52	53	54	55	56	57	58	59

C Match.

1. 

8:30

2. 

11:05

3. 

2:15

4. 

4:00

D Write.

1. 

8 : 1 0

2. 

___ : ___ ___

3. 

___ : ___ ___

4. 

___ : ___ ___

5. 

___ : ___ ___

6. 

___ : ___ ___

Lesson 2: Schedules

A Read. Write.

1. The office is open from ___8:30___ to ___6:00___.
2. The computer lab is open from ________ to ________.
3. The library is open from ________ to ________.

B Read. Write.

Class: 6:00 – 9:00
Break: 7:30 – 7:45

1. What time is class? It's ___from___ 6:00 ___to___ 9:00.
2. What time is break? It's ________ 7:30 ________ 7:45.

Class: 2:00 – 5:30
Break: 3:45 – 4:00

3. What time is class? It's ____________________.
4. What time is break? It's ____________________.

C Circle *Yes* or *No*.

Class: 1:00 – 4:00
Break: 2:15 – 2:30

1. Class is from 1:00 to 4:00. (Yes) No
2. Class starts at 1:00. Yes No
3. Class is over at 2:30. Yes No
4. Break starts at 2:15. Yes No
5. Break is over at 4:00. Yes No

D Read. Write.

Class: 8:00 – 11:30
Break: 9:45 – 10:00

from over starts to

1. Class is ___from___ 8:00 ___to___ 11:30.
2. Class ________ at 8:00.
3. Class is ________ at 11:30.
4. Break is ________ 9:45 ________ 10:00.
5. Break ________ at 9:45.
6. Break is ________ at 10:00.

Lesson 3: Daily activities

A Write.

get up
go to sleep

get up

get dressed
take a shower

4

eat breakfast
eat lunch

6

go to school
go to work

B T21 Listen. Check your answers.

C Write.

eat	get	go

1. get up
2. ________ dressed
3. ________ breakfast
4. ________ to work
5. ________ lunch
6. ________ to school
7. ________ home
8. ________ to sleep

D Write about you. Copy.

1. I get up at __:__. ____________________
2. I eat breakfast at __:__. ____________________
3. I eat lunch at __:__. ____________________
4. I go to school at __:__. ____________________
5. I go to sleep at __:__. ____________________

Lesson 4: Days of the week

A **Underline the word *day*.**

Sunday

Monday

Tuesday

Wednesday

Thursday

Friday

Saturday

B

Trace.	Copy.	Cover and write.
Sunday	Sunday	
Monday		
Tuesday		
Wednesday		
Thursday		
Friday		
Saturday		

C T22 Listen and circle.

1. Sunday Saturday
2. Wednesday Monday
3. Tuesday Thursday
4. Friday Wednesday
5. Thursday Tuesday
6. Monday Friday
7. Saturday Sunday

D Read. Write.

Sunday	Monday	Tuesday	Wednesday	Thursday	Friday	Saturday
Home	Work	School	Work	School	Work	Library

1. Tim is home on Sunday.
2. Tim goes to school on ______ and ______.
3. Tim goes to work on ______, ______, and ______.
4. Tim goes to the library on ______.

Lesson 5: Numbers 60–100

A Copy.

60	61	62	63	64	65	66	67	68	69
60									
70	71	72	73	74	75	76	77	78	79
70									
80	81	82	83	84	85	86	87	88	89
80									
90	91	92	93	94	95	96	97	98	99
90									
100									

B T23 Listen and circle.

1. 60 70 80 90 100
2. 60 70 80 90 100
3. 60 70 80 90 100
4. 60 70 80 90 100
5. 60 70 80 90 100

C T24 Listen and circle.

1. 12 20
2. 13 30
3. 14 40
4. 15 50
5. 16 60
6. 17 70
7. 18 80
8. 19 90

D T25 Listen. Write the time.

1. 2 : 0 0
2. ____ : __ __
3. ____ : __ __
4. ____ : __ __
5. ____ : __ __
6. ____ : __ __

Lesson 6: Carlo's story

A Listen and write.

T26

always	early	goes
late	~~on time~~	starts

1. Carlo likes to be ___on time___.
2. He gets up ______________ and gets ready for work.
3. He arrives at 6:50, and ______________ work at 7:00.
4. Carlo ______________ to school after work.
5. He is ______________ early for class.
6. But Carlo is always ______________ meeting friends!

B Write about you.

early	on time	late

1. I get to class ______________.
2. I get to work ______________.

Phonics

A T27 **Listen and write.** **Copy.**

t d

1. __inner ____________
2. __o ____________
3. __eacher ____________
4. __ay ____________
5. __ime ____________
6. __o ____________

B T28 **Listen and write.** **Copy.**

F M T Th S W

1. S aturday Saturday
2. __onday ____________
3. __ursday ____________
4. __ednesday ____________
5. __riday ____________
6. __unday ____________
7. __uesday ____________

Unit 4: Family and Friends

Lesson 1: Family

Write.

father
mother

1 ________________

2 ________________

son
daughter

3 ________________

4 ________________

sister
brother

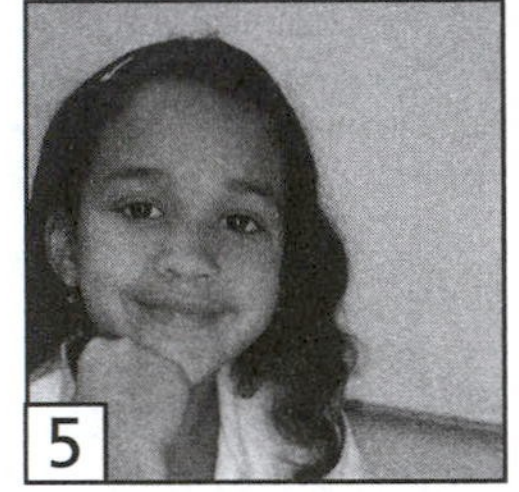

5 ________________

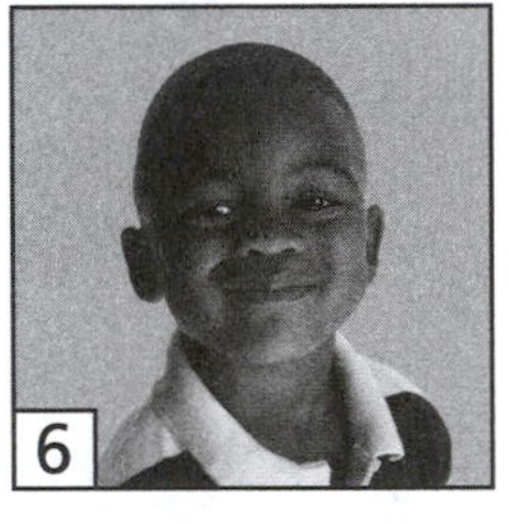

6 ________________

B Underline *er*.

sister brother mother father daughter

C Write.

grandfather
grandmother

______

______

wife
husband

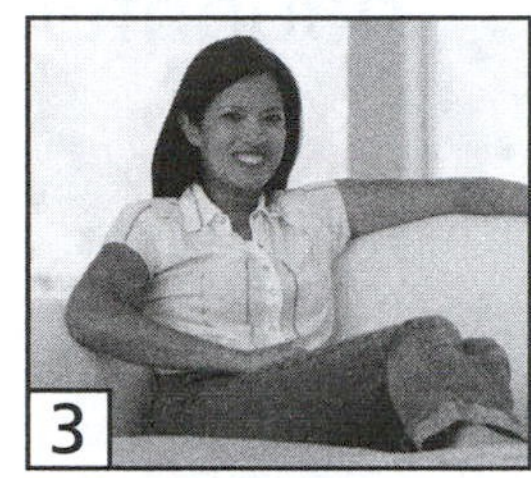

______

______

parents
children

______

______

D T29 Listen and circle.

1. (sister) son
2. brother mother
3. grandfather grandmother
4. daughter father
5. parents children
6. husband wife

A Circle the same.

1.	**mothers**	mother	brother	mothers
2.	**fathers**	father	fathers	fatter
3.	**daughters**	danger	daughter	daughters
4.	**sons**	suns	sons	son
5.	**brothers**	brother	brothers	bothers
6.	**sisters**	sister	mister	sisters
7.	**parents**	parents	apparent	parent
8.	**children**	child	children	childhood

B Write.

Singular	Plural
son	sons
daughter	______
father	______
mother	______
child	______
parent	______

C Read.

Antonio and his family

D Write.

children	family	~~married~~	wife

1. Antonio is ___married___.
2. This is his ______________.
3. Antonio has a ______________.
4. Antonio has three ______________.

E Circle *Yes* or *No* about you.

I am married.	Yes	No
I have children.	Yes	No
I have brothers.	Yes	No
I have sisters.	Yes	No

F Copy your *Yes* sentences in your notebook.

Lesson 3: Household chores

A **Write.**

do
vacuum

1

vacuum

2

________ the laundry

take out
wash

3

________ the garbage

4

________ the dishes

clean
make

5

________ dinner

6

________ the house

B T30 **Listen. Check your answers.**

C Write.

make	makes
do	does
wash	washes
take	takes
clean	cleans
vacuum	vacuums

1. I __________ dinner.
2. My mother __________ the laundry.
3. My daughter __________ the dishes.
4. My son __________ out the garbage.
5. I __________ the house.
6. My father __________.

D Circle *Yes* or *No* about you.

I clean the house.	Yes	No
I do the laundry.	Yes	No
I make dinner.	Yes	No
I take out the garbage.	Yes	No
I wash the dishes.	Yes	No
I vacuum.	Yes	No

E Copy your *Yes* sentences in your notebook.

Lesson 4: Months

A T31 **Listen and point.**

B

Trace.	Copy.	Cover and write.
January	January	
February		
March		
April		
May		
June		
July		
August		
September		
October		
November		
December		

Lesson 5: Write dates

A **Write.**

April	August	December
~~January~~	May	September

1. January
2. February
3. March
4. __________
5. __________
6. June
7. July
8. __________
9. __________
10. October
11. November
12. __________

B T31 **Listen. Check your answers.**

C T32 **Listen and circle.**

1. (January) June
2. May March
3. November December
4. July January
5. April August
6. September November

D Match.

1. March 7, 1969	7/3/59
2. July 3, 1959	3/7/69
3. October 6, 2012	10/6/12
4. June 10, 2011	6/10/11
5. September 4, 2011	4/9/14
6. April 9, 2014	9/4/11

E Write.

	Month / Day / Year
1. May 6, 1975	5 / 6 / 75
2. February 8, 1989	____ / ____ / ____
3. August 3, 2007	____ / ____ / ____
4. October 14, 2016	____ / ____ / ____
5. December 31, 2013	____ / ____ / ____
6. November 5, 1992	____ / ____ / ____

F Write.

What is your date of birth? ____ / ____ / ____

A Read.

Adult Education Center

Name	Mark	Don	Smith
	First	Middle	Last
Date of Birth	6/1/86		
Place of Birth	United States		

B Write.

first	last	1. His <u>first</u> name is Mark.
first	middle	2. His ________ name is Don.
middle	last	3. His ________ name is Smith.
date	birth	4. His ________ of birth is June 1, 1986.
date	birth	5. His place of ________ is the U.S.

C Write about you.

Name ______________________________

First   Last

Date of Birth ______________________________

Place of Birth ______________________________

A T33 Listen and write.

country	does	go	goes
helps	married	men	women

1. Ernesto and Maria are ____________.
2. In their country, ____________ go to work.
3. ____________ stay at home.
4. In their ____________, women do all the household chores.
5. In the United States, they both ____________ to work.
6. Ernesto ____________ at home.
7. He ____________ the dishes.
8. He ____________ to the supermarket.

A Listen and write. Copy.

T34

b d m n p

1. __iddle ____________
2. __irth ____________
3. __ate ____________
4. __lace ____________
5. __other ____________
6. __ame ____________
7. __aughter ____________
8. __arents ____________

B Listen and write. Copy.

T35

D M N

1. __arch ____________
2. __ay ____________
3. __ovember ____________
4. __ecember ____________

Unit 5: How much is it?

Lesson 1: U.S. coins

A **Match.**

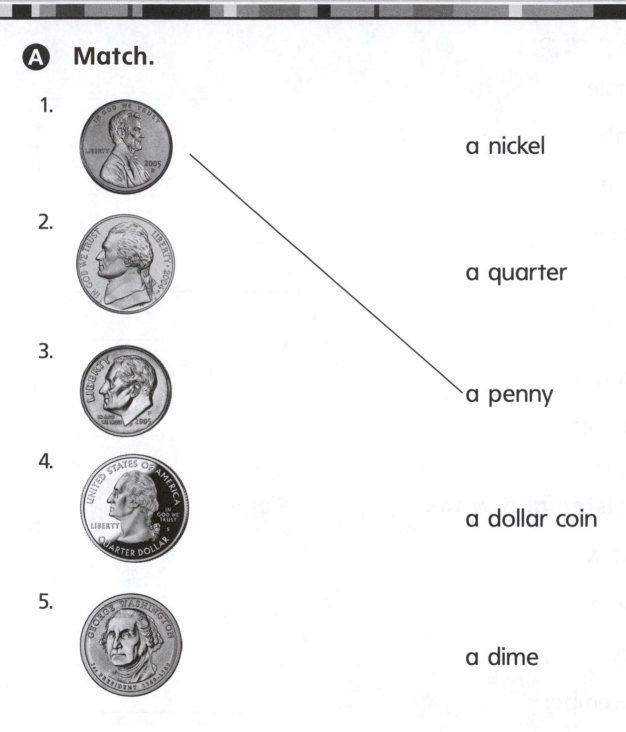

1.	a nickel
2.	a quarter
3.	a penny
4.	a dollar coin
5.	a dime

B T36 **Listen. Check your answers.**

C Circle the same amount.

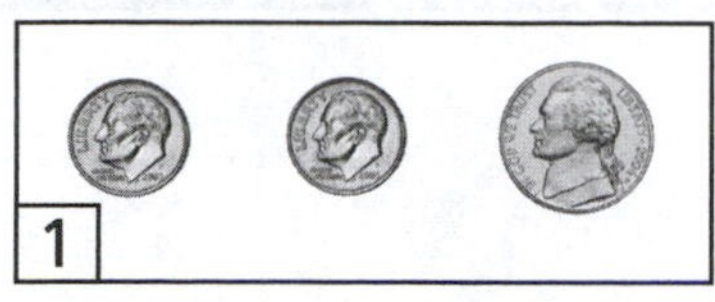

2 dimes and 1 nickel

1 dime and 2 nickels

2 quarters, 1 dime, and 3 nickels

3 quarters, 2 dimes, and 1 nickel

2 pennies and 5 dimes

2 quarters and 5 dimes

D Circle the answer.

Do you have change for a dollar?

Yes, I do. No, I don't.

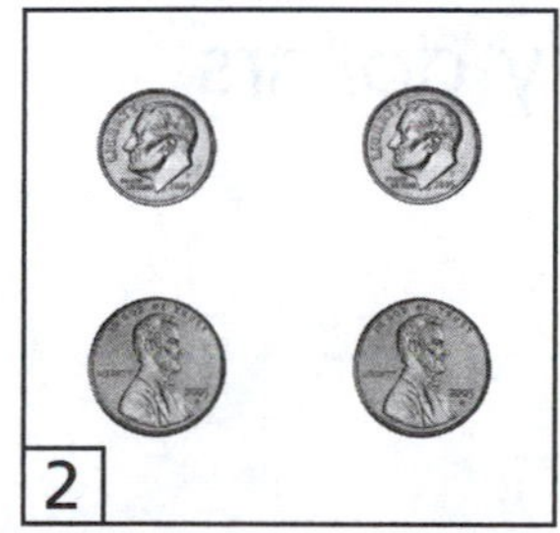

Do you have change for a quarter?

Yes, I do. No, I don't.

Do you have change for a dime?

Yes, I do. No, I don't.

A Match.

1. 

2. 

3. 

4. 

5. 

6. 

five dollars

ten dollars

one dollar

one hundred dollars

twenty dollars

fifty dollars

B T37 Listen. Check your answers.

C Trace. Copy. Cover and write.

1. one __________ __________
2. five __________ __________
3. ten __________ __________
4. twenty __________ __________
5. fifty __________ __________
6. one hundred __________ __________

D Circle the answer.

1. 

Do you have change for a ten?

Yes, I do. No, I don't.

2. Do you have change for a twenty?

Yes, I do. No, I don't.

3. 

Do you have change for a fifty?

Yes, I do. No, I don't.

4. 

Do you have change for a hundred?

Yes, I do. No, I don't.

A Write.

batteries soap

1 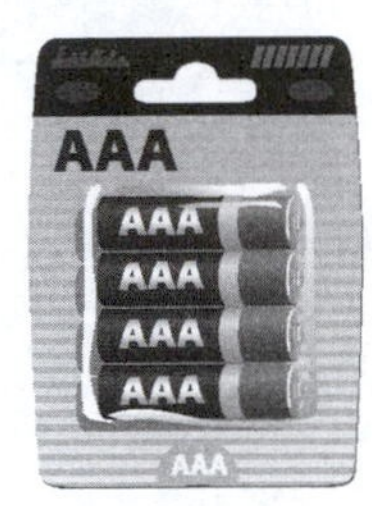

batteries

2 

______

lightbulbs toilet paper

3 

______

4 

______

tissues toothpaste

5 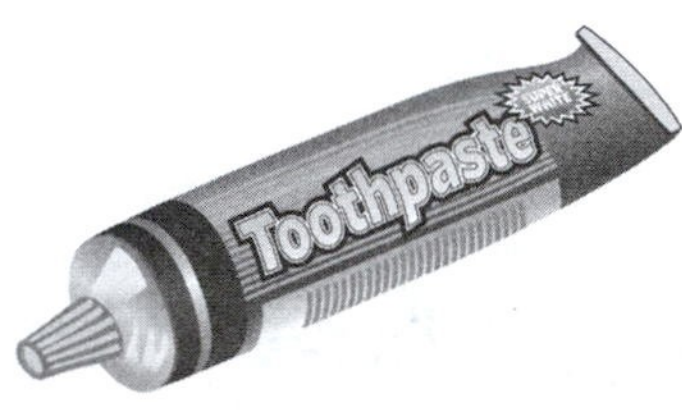

______

6 

______

paper towels razor blades

7 

______

8 

______

B T38 Listen. Check your answers.

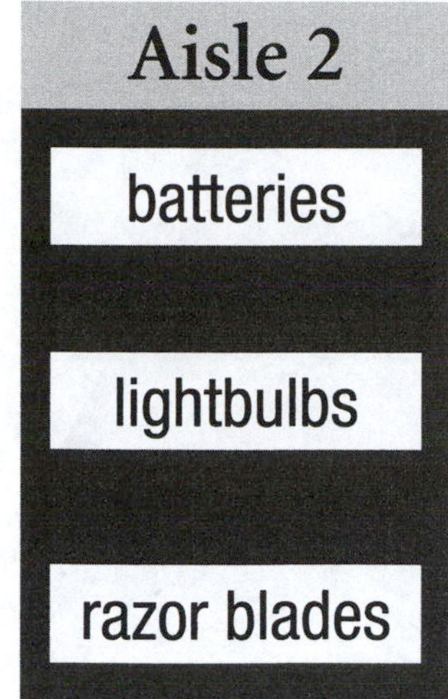

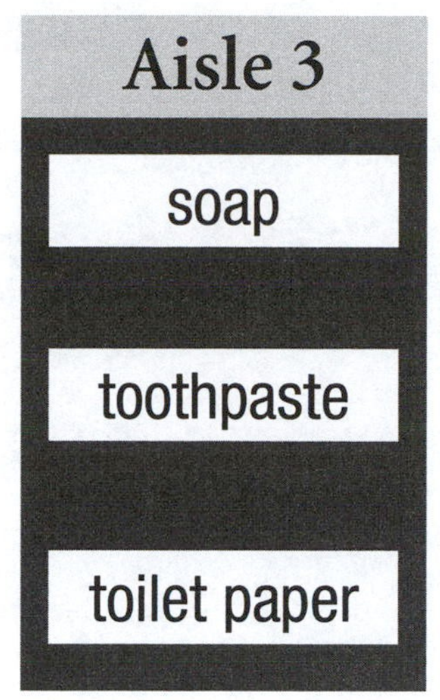

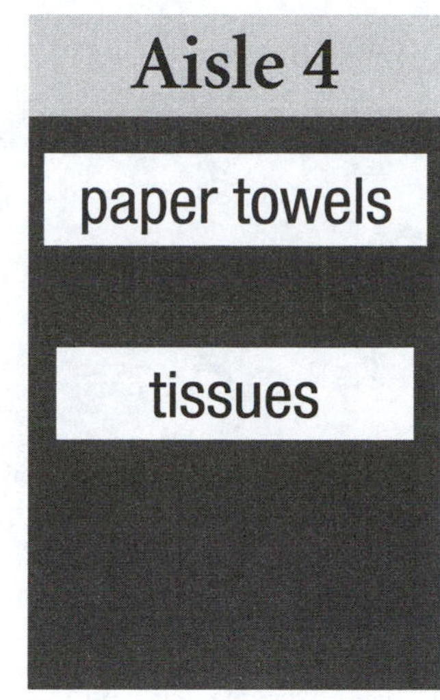

C Write.

1. Where is the soap? Aisle 3.
2. Where are the paper towels? Aisle __.
3. Where are the lightbulbs? Aisle __.

D Write.

is	are

1. Where are the tissues? Aisle 4.
2. Where ______ the toothpaste? Aisle 3.
3. Where ______ razor blades? Aisle 2.
4. Where ______ the toilet paper? Aisle 3.
5. Where ______ batteries? Aisle 2.

Lesson 4: Prices

A Look. Trace. Copy.

1. $ 1.00 ______

2. $ 5.10 ______

3. $10.25 ______

4. $10.05 ______

5. $20.20 ______

B T39 Listen and circle.

1. $ 1.59 $ 11.59
2. $ 8.64 $86.49
3. $ 7.28 $72.80
4. $15.63 $59.63
5. $ 5.40 $95.40
6. $ 2.15 $32.15

C Write.

1.  $10.20

2.     ______

3.    ______

4.    ______

5.    ______

Lesson 5: Receipts

A Circle the same words in the receipt.

~~ABC Drugstore~~	Batteries	Lightbulbs
Paper towels	Soap	Toothpaste

ABC Drugstore

Date: 4/9/13

1	Lightbulbs	$ 4.20
2	Soap	4.50
1	Paper towels	3.25
2	Batteries	9.00
1	Razor blades	10.49
1	Toothpaste	2.89
	Subtotal	$ 34.33
	Tax	1.72
	Total	$ 36.05

Total items = 8

B Read the receipt. Circle *Yes* or *No*.

1. The receipt is from ABC Drugstore. Yes No
2. The batteries are $19.00. Yes No
3. The lightbulbs are $4.02. Yes No
4. The toothpaste is $2.89. Yes No
5. The paper towels are $3.25. Yes No
6. The soap is $4.50. Yes No

C Circle the same words in the receipt.

Date	items	Subtotal	Tax	Total

City Drugstore

Date: 10/21/14

4	Toilet paper	$ 3.96
2	Tissues	4.00
1	Soap	1.50
Subtotal		$ 9.46
Tax		.47
Total		$ 9.93

Total items = 7

D Read the receipt. Write.

1. The receipt is from City Drugstore.
2. The date is ______________________.
3. The subtotal is ______________________.
4. The tax is ______________________.
5. The total is ______________________.
6. The total number of items is ______________________.

Lesson 6: Edna's story

A T40 Listen and write.

buy	get	is	pay	shop	talk

1. My name ____________ Edna.
2. I ____________ at markets.
3. I ____________ about the prices.
4. I ____________ good bargains.
5. I ____________ in big stores.
6. I ____________ the price on the price tag.
7. I ____________ things on sale.

B Circle *Yes* or *No* about you.

I shop at markets.	Yes	No
I talk about the prices.	Yes	No
I shop in big stores.	Yes	No
I buy things on sale.	Yes	No

Phonics

A T41 Listen and write. Copy.

c g

1. __oin ____________
2. __o ____________
3. __et ____________
4. __ood ____________
5. __ountry ____________
6. __ost ____________

B T42 Listen and write. Copy.

d b

1. __ime ____________
2. __argain ____________
3. __uy ____________
4. __ollar ____________
5. __atteries ____________
6. __ate ____________

Unit 6: Let's eat!

Lesson 1: Vegetables

A T43 **Listen and point.**

B **Trace and copy.**

1 onions

2 cucumbers

3 tomatoes

4 peas

5 mushrooms

6 peppers

7 lettuce

8 potatoes

9 carrots

C Read. Underline the vegetables.

Karen wants to make vegetable soup.
She has onions.
She has potatoes and peas.
She needs carrots and peppers.
She goes to the store.
She buys carrots and peppers.
She makes the soup.
It's good!

D What is in Karen's soup? Write.

Karen's soup has ___onions___, ______________,

______________, ______________, and peppers.

E What's in your favorite soup? Write.

My favorite soup has ______________________________

____

____.

Lesson 2: Vegetables

A T44 **Listen and circle.**

1. onions cucumbers
2. potatoes tomatoes
3. carrots lettuce
4. peppers mushrooms
5. cucumbers carrots
6. peppers peas
7. tomatoes mushrooms
8. peppers potatoes

B T45 **Listen and circle.**

1. like don't like
2. like don't like
3. like don't like
4. like don't like
5. like don't like
6. like don't like

C Write the sentences. Use contractions.

1. I do not like carrots. I don't like carrots.
2. They do not like cucumbers. ______
3. We do not like peppers. ______
4. I do not like tomatoes. ______
5. They do not like peas. ______
6. We do not like onions. ______

D Write about you.

like	don't like

1. I ______ vegetables.
2. I ______ peppers.
3. I ______ potatoes.
4. I ______ onions.
5. I ______ cucumbers.
6. I ______ tomatoes.
7. I ______ mushrooms.
8. I ______ peas.

Lesson 3: Fruit

A Write.

banana
peaches

1 peaches

2 ____________

oranges
pears

3 ____________

4 ____________

cherries
strawberries

5 ____________

6 ____________

apples
grapes

7 ____________

8 ____________

B T46 Listen. Check your answers.

C Write.

	Fruit	Vegetable
1. carrots / cherries	cherries	______
2. bananas / onions	______	______
3. peas / peaches	______	______
4. oranges / potatoes	______	______

D Read.

My name is Liz. I like fruit. I like apples and pears. I like some vegetables. I don't like peas or carrots.

E Write.

likes doesn't like

1. Liz ______ fruit.
2. She ______ some vegetables.
3. Liz ______ apples and pears.
4. She ______ peas.
5. She ______ carrots.

Lesson 4: Food amounts

Write.

bread
milk

1 milk

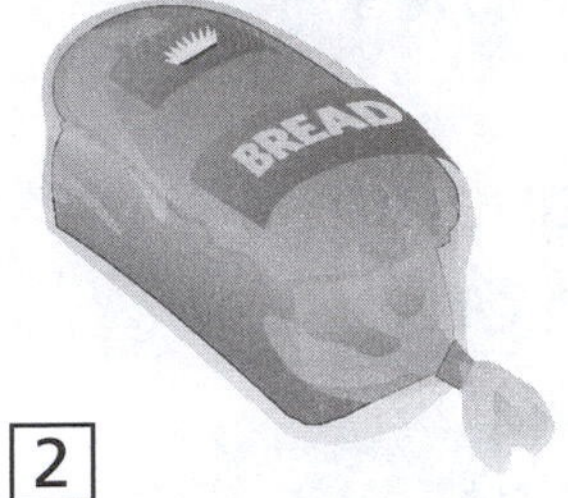

2 ____________

cereal
eggs

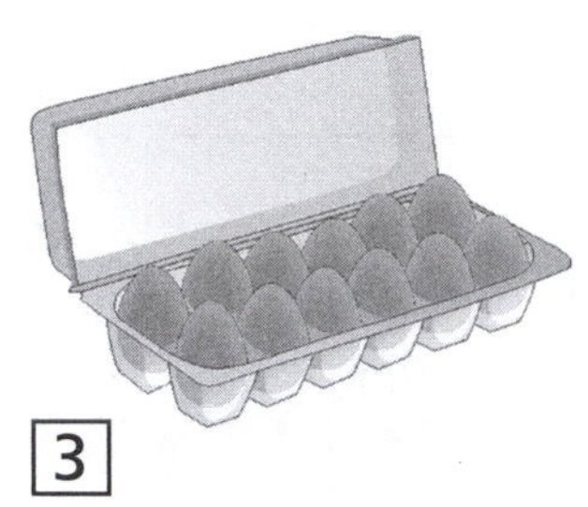

3 ____________

4 ____________

chicken
fish

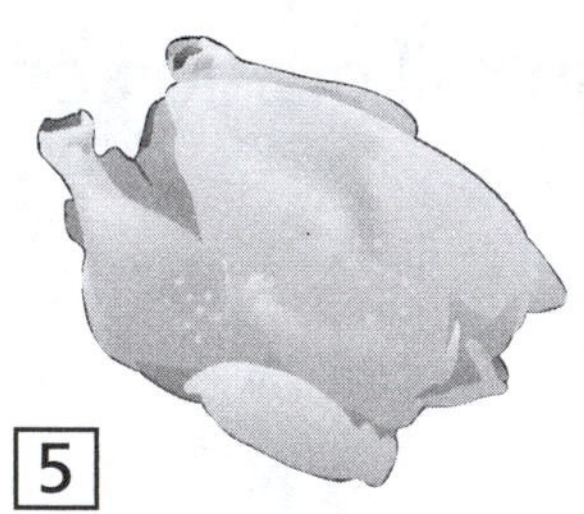

5 ____________

6 ____________

rice
soup

7 ____________

8 ____________

T47

Listen. Check your answers.

C Read. Underline the words *pound* and *pounds*.

lb. = pound
lbs. = pounds

Pat and Fred are at the store.
They need two pounds of rice.
They need one pound of fish.
They need three pounds of chicken.
They need four pounds of grapes.

D Write.

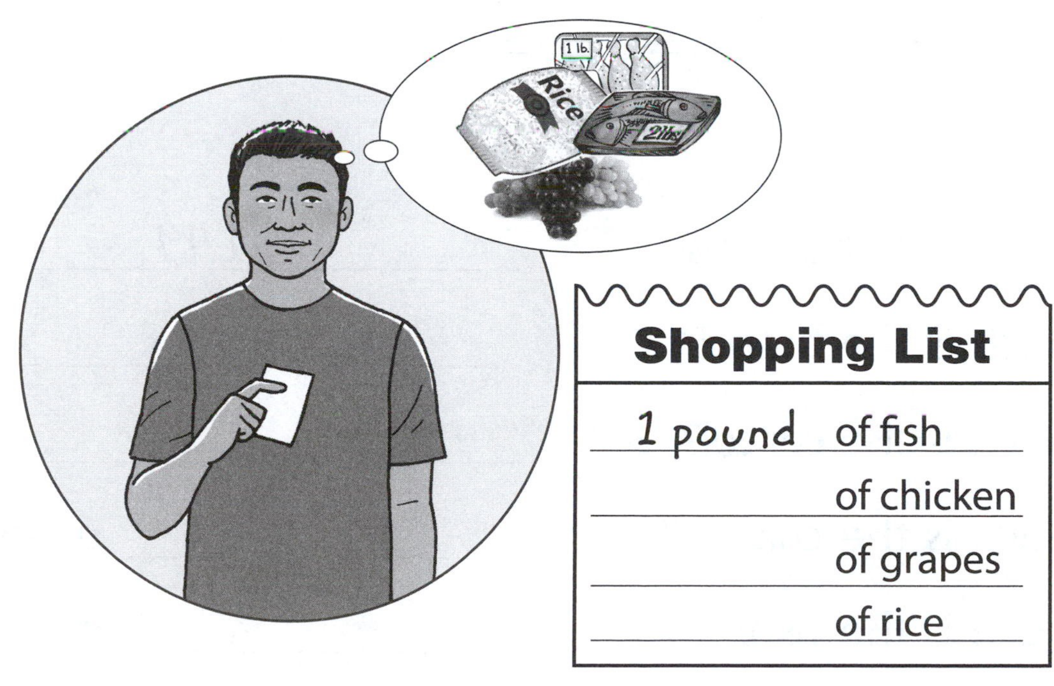

Shopping List

1 pound of fish
_______ of chicken
_______ of grapes
_______ of rice

A **Read the ad. Circle the prices.**

Shop Mart Weekly Specials
Bread $3.99
BREAD
Rice $5.69
Rice
Fish $6.99/lb
2lbs
Chicken $2.29/lb
Eggs $1.49
Cereal $3.75
Corn Flakes
Milk $3.89
Milk
Soup $1.20
SOUP
SOUP

B **Write.**

1. How much are the eggs? $1.49
2. How much is the bread? ______
3. How much is the cereal? ______
4. How much is the chicken? ______ a pound
5. How much is the fish? ______ a pound

Lesson 6: A menu

A **Read. Circle three things you want for lunch.**

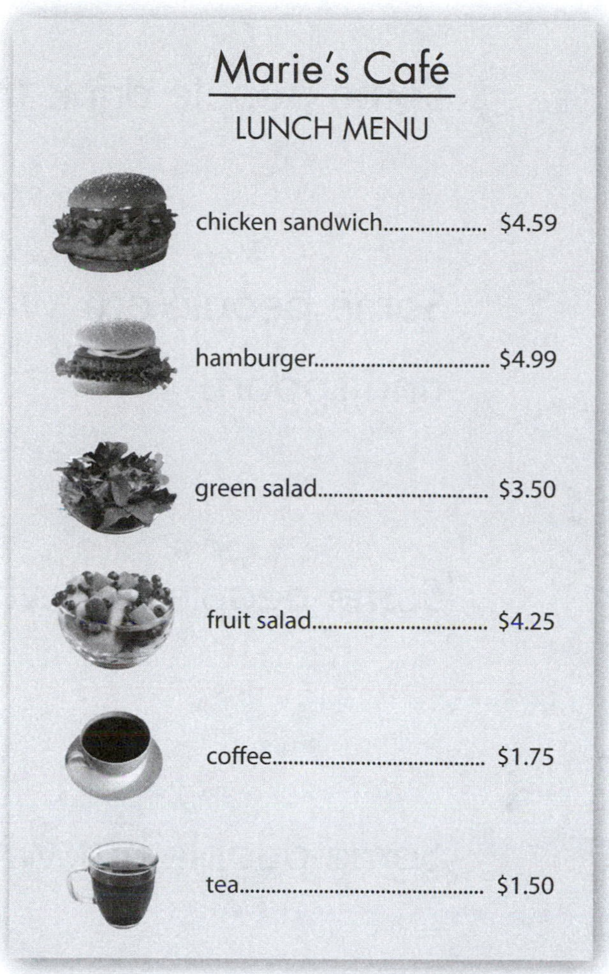

Marie's Café
LUNCH MENU
chicken sandwich.................. $4.59
hamburger.............................. $4.99
green salad............................ $3.50
fruit salad............................. $4.25
coffee.................................... $1.75
tea... $1.50

B **Write your order.**

I'd like ______________________________, and

______________________________, and

______________________________.

Lesson 7: Tran's story

A Match.

Some people drink their soup.

Some people eat with forks, knives, and spoons.

Some people eat with their fingers.

Some people eat with chopsticks.

B T48 Listen. Check your answers.

C Circle *Yes* or *No* about you.

1. I eat sandwiches with my fingers. Yes No
2. I eat soup with a spoon. Yes No
3. I eat rice with chopsticks. Yes No

A Listen and write. Copy.

T49

f s v

1. __oup ____________________
2. __ish ____________________
3. __egetable ____________________
4. __ood ____________________
5. __ruit ____________________
6. __alad ____________________
7. __ingers ____________________

B Listen and write. Copy.

T50

c ch

1. __arrots ____________________
2. __icken ____________________
3. __ucumbers ____________________
4. __erries ____________________
5. lun__ ____________________
6. sandwi__ ____________________

Unit 7: Apartments for Rent

Lesson 1: Rooms in a home

A Match.

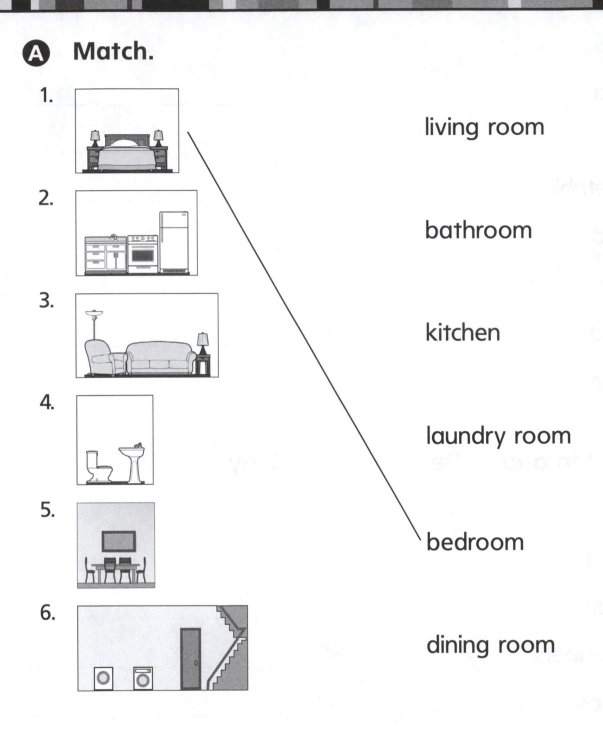

1.  living room
2. bathroom
3. kitchen
4. laundry room
5. bedroom
6. dining room

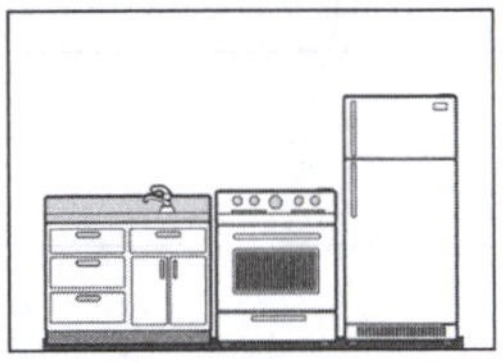

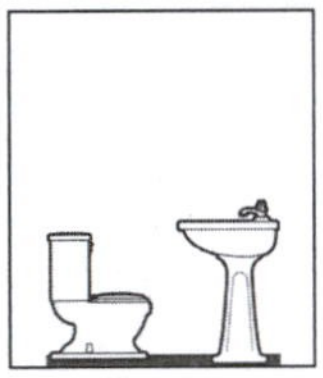

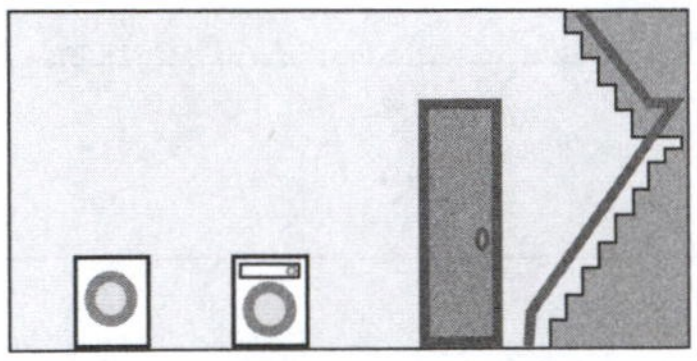

B Listen. Check your answers.

C **Write.** **Copy.**

b l d r

1. r oom room
2. __edroom ______________
3. __iving __oom ______________
4. __athroom ______________
5. __aundry __oom ______________
6. __ining __oom ______________
7. apa__tment ______________

D **Write.**

~~bathroom~~	~~dining room~~	bedroom
kitchen	laundry room	living room

One word	**Two words**
bathroom	dining room
______________	______________
______________	______________

Lesson 2: Talking about an apartment

A Look. Circle *Yes* or *No*.

1. There is a kitchen. (Yes) No
2. There is a laundry room. Yes No
3. There is a dining room. Yes No
4. There is a living room. Yes No
5. There are three bedrooms. Yes No
6. There are two bathrooms. Yes No

B Write.

is are

1. There ________ a bathroom.
2. There ________ two bathrooms.
3. There ________ one bedroom.
4. There ________ three bedrooms.

C Write.

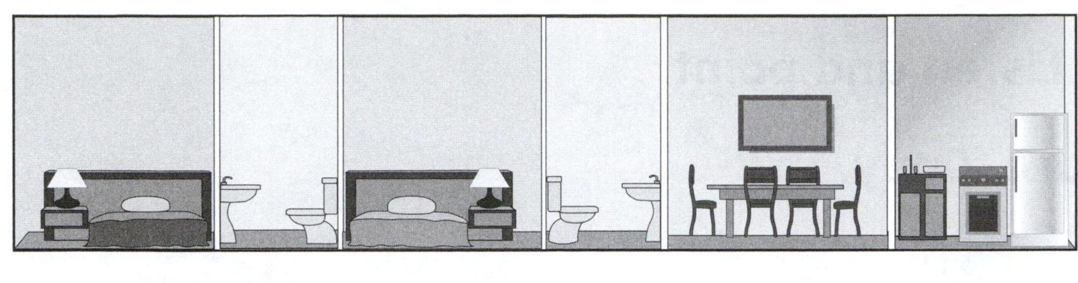

is are

1. There is a kitchen.
2. There ________ two bedrooms.
3. There ________ a dining room.
4. There ________ two bathrooms.

D Write about your home.

1. There is a ________________.
2. There is a ________________.
3. There are ________________.
4. There are ________________.

Lesson 3: Furniture and appliances

A T52 **Listen and point.**

B **Trace. Copy.**

1 chair

2 table

3 lamp

4 dresser

5 sofa

6 bed

7 dishwasher

8 stove

9 refrigerator

C Write.

Yes, there is.
No, there isn't.

1. Is there a chair? No, there isn't.
2. Is there a stove? ____________
3. Is there a bed? ____________
4. Is there a refrigerator? ____________
5. Is there a table? ____________

D Write.

Yes, there are.
No, there aren't.

1. Are there any tables? ____________
2. Are there any beds? ____________
3. Are there any dishwashers? ____________
4. Are there any sofas? ____________

Lesson 4: An address

A T53 Listen and circle.

1.	3	13	30
2.	4	14	40
3.	5	15	50
4.	6	16	60
5.	7	17	70
6.	8	18	80

B T54 Listen and circle.

1.	30 River Drive	30 River Road
2.	88 Lake Street	88 Lake Boulevard
3.	60 Park Lane	60 Park Avenue
4.	14 Bank Street	14 Bank Drive
5.	75 North Avenue	75 North Road
6.	19 City Lane	19 City Boulevard

C T55 Listen and circle.

1. 75 755
2. 217 270
3. 86 836
4. 24 240
5. 33 330

D Read. Write.

34 Park ______________

527 Lake ______________

1498 Bank ______________

910 River ______________

14 Cherry ______________

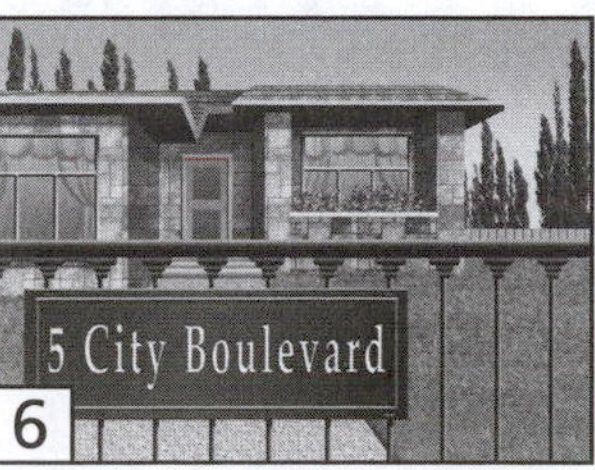

5 City ______________

Lesson 5: Address an envelope

A Match.

1.	Street	Blvd.
2.	Avenue	St.
3.	Drive	Ave.
4.	Boulevard	Dr.
5.	Lane	Apt.
6.	Road	Rd.
7.	Apartment	Ln.

B Trace. Copy. Cover and write.

	Trace.	Copy.	Cover and write.
1.	Apt.	____________	____________
2.	Ave.	____________	____________
3.	Blvd.	____________	____________
4.	Dr.	____________	____________
5.	Ln.	____________	____________
6.	Rd.	____________	____________

C Tim Lee wants to send a letter to Ann White.

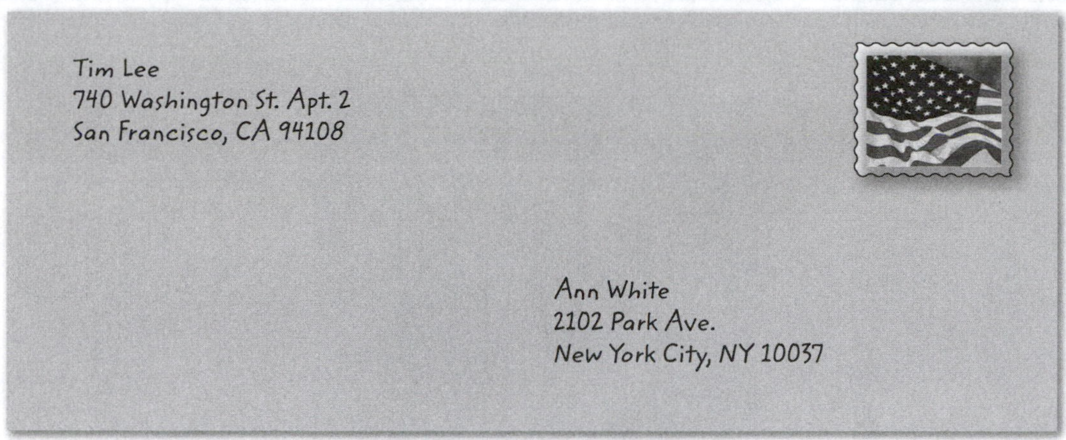

D Write.

from	to

1. The letter is __________ Tim Lee.
2. The letter is __________ Ann White.

E You want to send a letter to Tim Lee. Write.

____
Name

____
Address

__________ ____ __________
City State Zip code

____

____

__________ ____ __________

Lesson 6: Alicia's story

A T56 Listen and write.

12	21	1. Alicia is ________ years old.
single	married	2. She is ________.
sister	sisters	3. She lives with her ________ and her brother-in-law.
good	hard	4. Alicia has a ________ job.
parents	friends	5. She wants to live with her ________.
students	parents	6. Her ________ are not happy.
city	country	7. In their ________, single people live with family.

Phonics

A T57 **Listen and write.** **Copy.**

l r

1. __amp ______________________
2. __oom ______________________
3. __iving room ______________________
4. __ent ______________________
5. __oad ______________________
6. __aundry ______________________

B T58 **Listen and write.** **Copy.**

b d

1. __ed ______________________
2. __ining room ______________________
3. __athroom ______________________
4. __oulevard ______________________
5. __rive ______________________
6. __resser ______________________

Unit 8: Shopping

Lesson 1: Clothes and shoes

A T59 **Listen and point.**

B **Trace. Copy.**

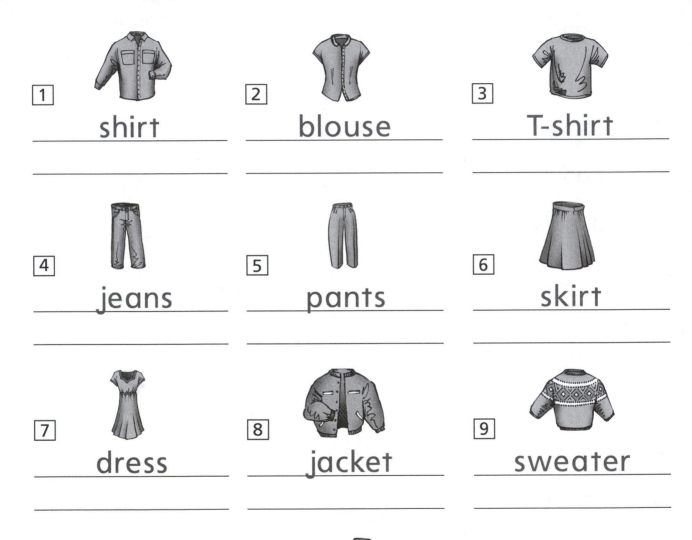

1 shirt

2 blouse

3 T-shirt

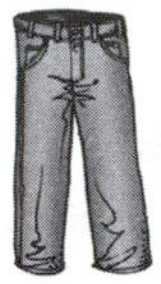

4 jeans

5 pants

6 skirt

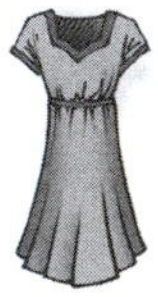

7 dress

8 jacket

9 sweater

10 shoes

11 socks

12 sneakers

C Write. Copy.

s j

1. s kirt — skirt
2. __ocks — ____________
3. __acket — ____________
4. __neakers — ____________
5. __eans — ____________

D Write.

~~blouse~~	jacket	jeans	~~pants~~	shirt
shoes	sneakers	socks	sweater	

Singular	Plural
blouse	pants
____________	____________
____________	____________
____________	____________
	____________

Lesson 2: Clothing sizes

A Match.

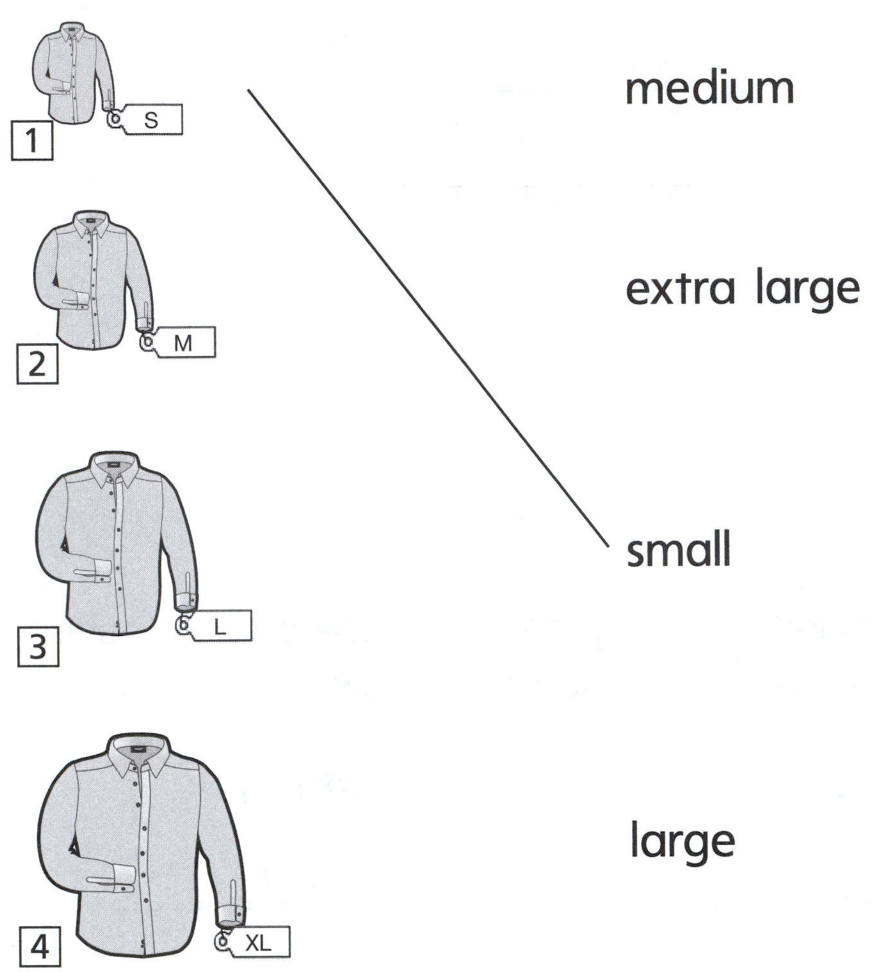

medium

extra large

small

large

B Write.

extra large	large	medium	small

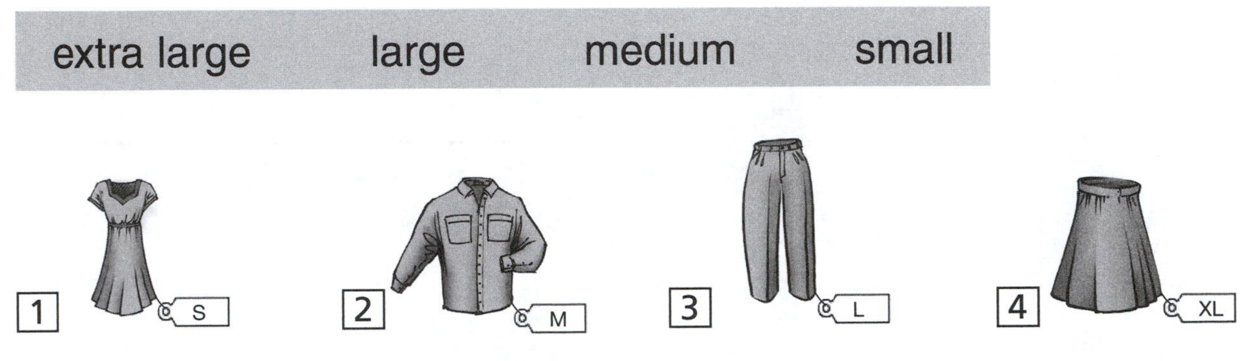

C Write.

blouse socks

1. Do you have this ___blouse___ in a small?
2. Do you have these ___________ in a large?

jacket shoes

3. Do you have this ___________ in a size 16?
4. Do you have these ___________ in a size 10?

D Write.

this these

1. Do you have ___these___ pants in a size 6?
2. Do you have ___________ shirt in a medium?
3. Do you have ___________ shoes in a size 8?
4. Do you have ___________ dress in a large?
5. Do you have ___________ sweater in a size 12?
6. Do you have ___________ jeans in a small?

Lesson 3: Colors

A T60 **Listen and write. Copy.**

b p g

1. b lue ______ blue
2. __ink ______
3. __ray ______
4. __eige ______
5. __urple ______
6. __rown ______
7. __reen ______
8. __lack ______

B **Trace.** **Copy.** **Cover and write.**

1. orange ______ ______
2. yellow ______ ______
3. white ______ ______
4. red ______ ______

C Match.

1. white + brown = orange
2. white + black = green
3. yellow + blue = beige
4. yellow + red = gray
5. white + red = purple
6. red + blue = pink

D Read. Underline the colors.

Jim is shopping.
He needs a gray sweater.
He needs black pants and a white shirt.
He needs brown shoes.
He needs blue socks.

E Read again. Circle *Yes* or *No*.

1. Jim needs gray pants. Yes No
2. He needs a white shirt. Yes No
3. Jim needs a black sweater. Yes No
4. He needs blue socks. Yes No
5. Jim needs black shoes. Yes No

Lesson 4: Return clothes

A Match.

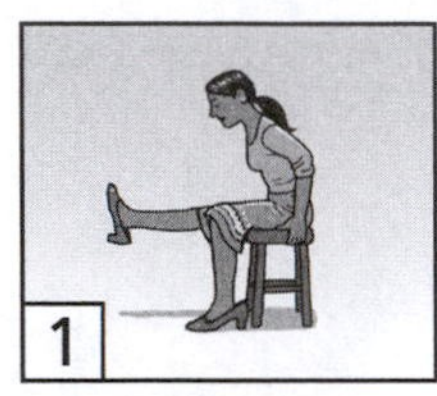

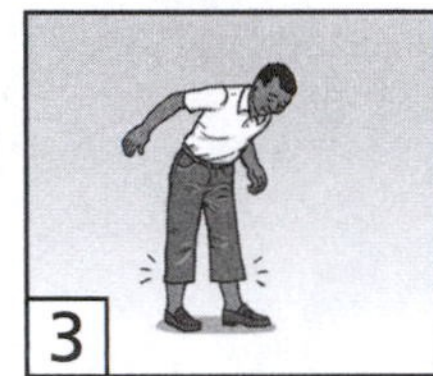

too small

too big

too long

too short

B Read.

Sam needs to return a sweater and some socks. The sweater is too long. The socks are too big. Sam has the receipt.

C Read again. Circle *Yes* or *No*.

1. Sam needs to return some clothes. Yes No
2. The sweater is too small. Yes No
3. The socks are too long. Yes No
4. Sam has the receipt. Yes No

D Write. Use *too*.

big	~~long~~	small	short

1. 

   What's the problem?

   The dress is too long.

2. 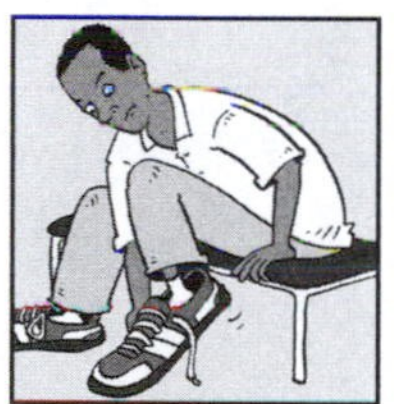

   What's the problem?

   The shoes are ________________.

3. 

   What's the problem?

   The jacket is ________________.

4. 

   What's the problem?

   The pants are ________________.

Lesson 5: Read a store ad

A **Read.**

Women's Clothing Sale
Regular price $80
ON SALE $59
Regular price $25
ON SALE $19
Regular price $49
ON SALE $35
Regular price $50
ON SALE $39

B **Write.**

regular	sale

1. The ______________ price for sweaters is $39.
2. The ______________ price for dresses is $80.
3. The ______________ price for skirts is $49.
4. The ______________ price for sweaters is $50.
5. The ______________ price for blouses is $19.
6. The ______________ price for dresses is $59.

C Read.

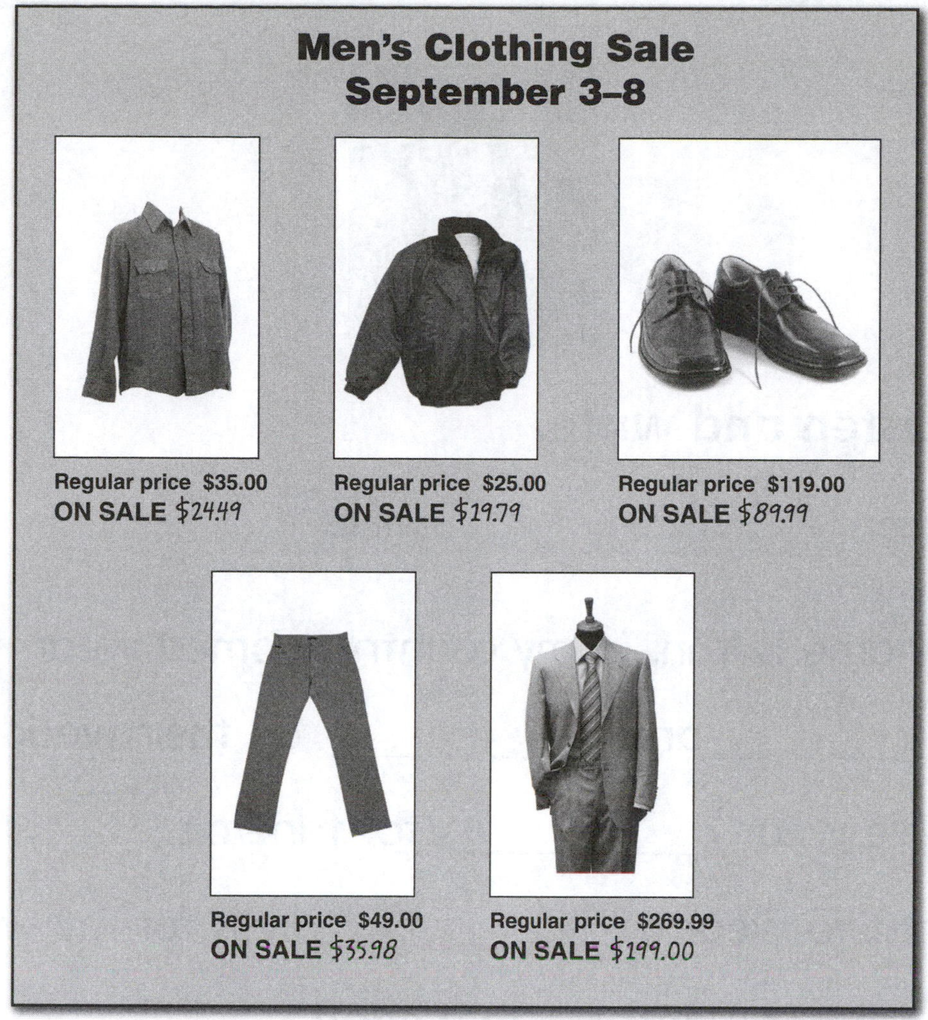

D Write.

1. What's the sale price for suits? $199.00
2. What's the regular price for pants? ____________
3. What's the sale price for shoes? ____________
4. What's the regular price for shirts? ____________
5. What's the regular price for suits? ____________
6. What's the sale price for jackets? ____________

A T61 **Listen and write.**

green	red	white

1. My name is Yun. In my country, women wear ____________ and ____________ on their wedding day.
2. People wear ____________ for funerals.
3. I want to wear a ____________ dress for my wedding.
4. My mother wants me to wear a ____________ and ____________ dress on my wedding day.

B **Write about colors in your country.**

1. Women wear ____________ on their wedding day.
2. Men wear ____________ on their wedding day.
3. People wear ____________ for funerals.

Phonics

A T62 **Listen and write.** **Copy.**

sh s

1. __ort ____________
2. __ale ____________
3. __irt ____________
4. __ize ____________
5. __ocks ____________
6. __oes ____________
7. __uit ____________
8. __opping ____________

B T63 **Listen and write.** **Copy.**

j g

1. __ray ____________
2. __eans ____________
3. __acket ____________
4. __reen ____________

Unit 9: Our Busy Lives

Lesson 1: What do you do in your free time?

A **Write.**

play
read

1 ___play___ the guitar

2 ________ the newspaper

listen to
watch

3 ________ TV

4 ________ music

exercise
go to

5 ________ the movies

6 ________

play
visit

7 ________ friends

8 ________ soccer

B  T64 **Listen. Check your answers.**

C Write about Tammy's free time.

friends	the guitar	~~music~~	the movies	TV

1. Tammy listens to ___music___.
2. She goes to ____________.
3. She plays ____________.
4. She watches ____________.
5. She visits ____________.

D Circle *Yes* or *No* about you.

I listen to music.	Yes	No
I play soccer.	Yes	No
I go to the movies.	Yes	No
I read the newspaper.	Yes	No
I exercise.	Yes	No
I watch TV.	Yes	No
I visit friends.	Yes	No
I play the guitar.	Yes	No

E Copy your *Yes* sentences in your notebook.

Lesson 2: Are you busy?

A T65 Listen and circle.

1. playing going
2. reading watching
3. exercising visiting
4. reading playing
5. visiting listening
6. going reading

B Write.

listening	playing	reading	~~shopping~~	visiting

1. My family is shopping today.
2. My son is ____________ soccer.
3. My wife is ____________ friends.
4. My daughter is ____________ a book.
5. I am ____________ to music.

C Write.

is are

1. They ___are___ exercising.
2. She ________ playing soccer.
3. We ________ visiting friends.
4. You ________ watching TV.

D Circle the contractions.

1. You are (You're)
2. He is He's
3. They are They're
4. We're We are

E Write the sentences. Use contractions.

1. You are exercising. You're exercising.
2. He is reading a book. ________________
3. She is visiting friends. ________________
4. We are listening to music. ________________
5. They are playing soccer. ________________

Lesson 3: Are you doing homework?

A **Write.**

doing talking

1 doing homework

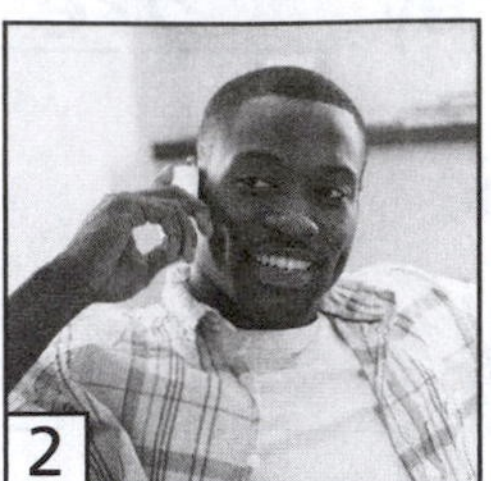

2 __________ on the phone

making taking out

3 __________ dinner

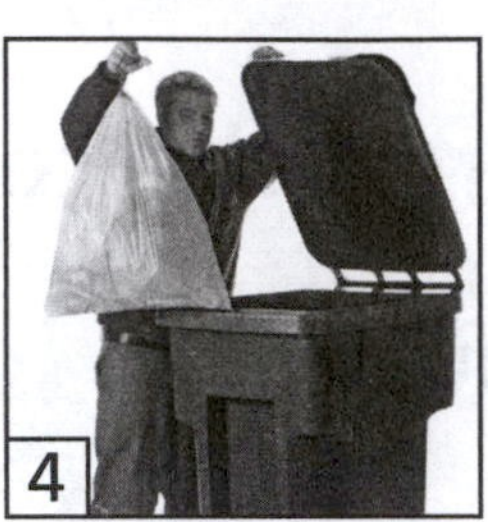

4 __________ the garbage

doing paying

5 __________ bills

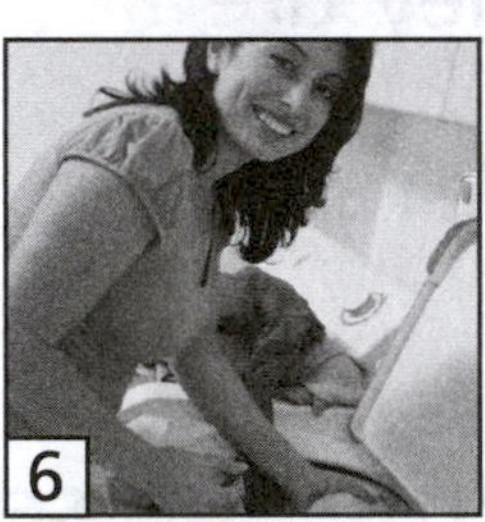

6 __________ the laundry

walking washing

7 __________ the car

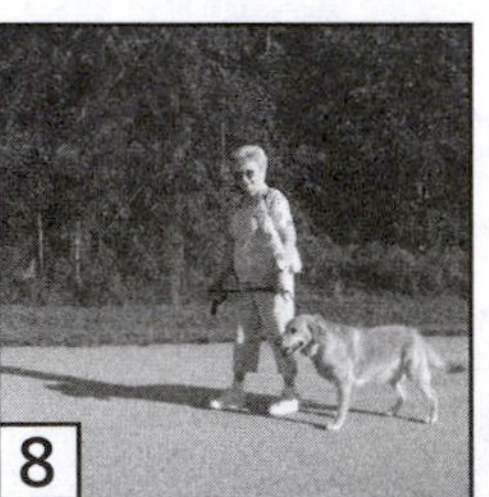

8 __________ the dog

B T66 **Listen. Check your answers.**

C Look and write.

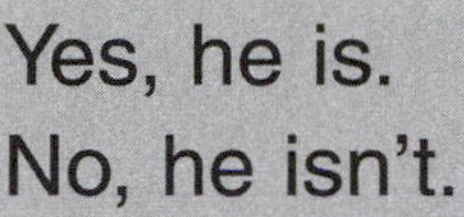

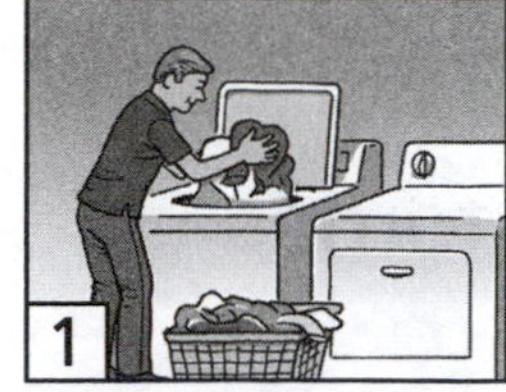

1. Is he doing laundry? Yes, he is.

2. Is he vacuuming? ______________________

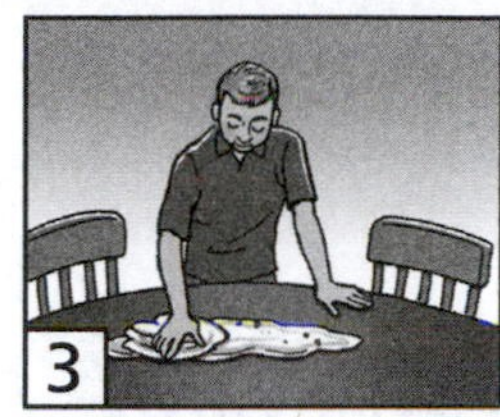

3. Is he paying bills? ______________________

4. Is he making dinner? ______________________

5. Is he washing the dishes? ______________________

6. Is he walking the dog? ______________________

Ⓐ Match.

1. 

2. 

3. 

4. 

5. 

He's helping a customer.

He's fixing cars.

He's looking for something.

He's taking orders.

She's taking a break.

Ⓑ T67 Listen. Check your answers.

Ⓒ Look. Write *not* and ✔.

She's __not__ fixing cars.

She's __✔__ driving a truck.

They're ______ counting money.

They're ______ taking a break.

He's ______ taking orders on the phone.

He's ______ working on a computer.

Ⓓ Write sentences. Use a capital letter and a period.

1. they're not fixing the car they're washing the car

   They're not fixing the car. They're washing the car.

2. she's not doing homework she's paying the bills

   ____

3. he's working on the computer he's not talking on the phone

   ____

Lesson 5: Write a phone message

A Read. Circle *Yes* or *No*.

MESSAGE

For: Ms. Brown Date: May 4

Caller: Tom Wilson Phone: 203-555-1234

Message: He's not coming to class today.

1. The message is for Ms. Brown. Yes No
2. The message is from Tom Wilson. Yes No
3. Tom Wilson is coming to class today. Yes No

B Read. Write the message.

The message is for Mr. Peters.

The caller is Meg Adams.

Meg is coming to work late.

MESSAGE

For: Mr. Peters Date: October 15

Caller: ______ Phone: 510-555-6789

Message: ______

C T68 Listen. Circle the message.

1. She's coming to work late today.

   She's not coming to work today.

2. He's driving to work today.

   He's not driving to work today.

3. They're coming to school late today.

   They're not coming to school today.

D T69 Listen. Write the message.

MESSAGE	
For: Mr. Green	Date: January 21
Caller: Sam Elder	Phone: 219-555-6745
Message: He's	

E T70 Listen. Write the message.

MESSAGE	
For: Ms. Smith	Date: December 4
Caller: Kate Lin	Phone: 503-555-2941
Message: She's	

Lesson 6: Alfonso's story

T71

A **Listen and write.**

busy	eat	go	~~is~~
play	sit	spend	talk

1. My name ___is___ Alfonso.
2. Every weekend, my children are ________ with their friends.
3. They ________ on the phone with their friends.
4. They ________ shopping with their friends.
5. They ________ sports with their friends.
6. In my country, children ________ time with their family on the weekends.
7. They ________ dinner with their family.
8. They ________ and talk with their family.

B **Write about you.**

I spend time with ____________ on the weekend.

Phonics

A T72 **Listen and write.** **Copy.**

ay

1. pl____ ______________________
2. p____ ______________________
3. d____ ______________________
4. aw____ ______________________

B T73 **Listen and write.** **Copy.**

e

1. y__s ______________________
2. h__llo ______________________
3. y__llow ______________________
4. h__lp ______________________

C T74 **Listen. Circle the words with the same end sound.**

1.	 take	 make	talk
2.	late	last	date
3.	red	read	bed
4.	ten	pen	tea

Unit 10: Where's the bus stop?

Lesson 1: Places in the community

A Write.

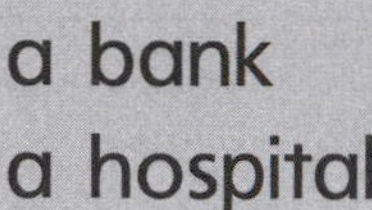

a bank
a hospital

____

____

a gas station
a parking lot

____

____

a restaurant
a supermarket

____

____

an ATM
a drugstore

____

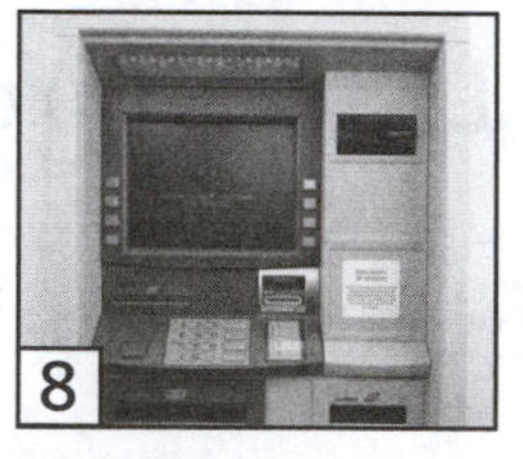

____

B T75 **Listen. Check your answers.**

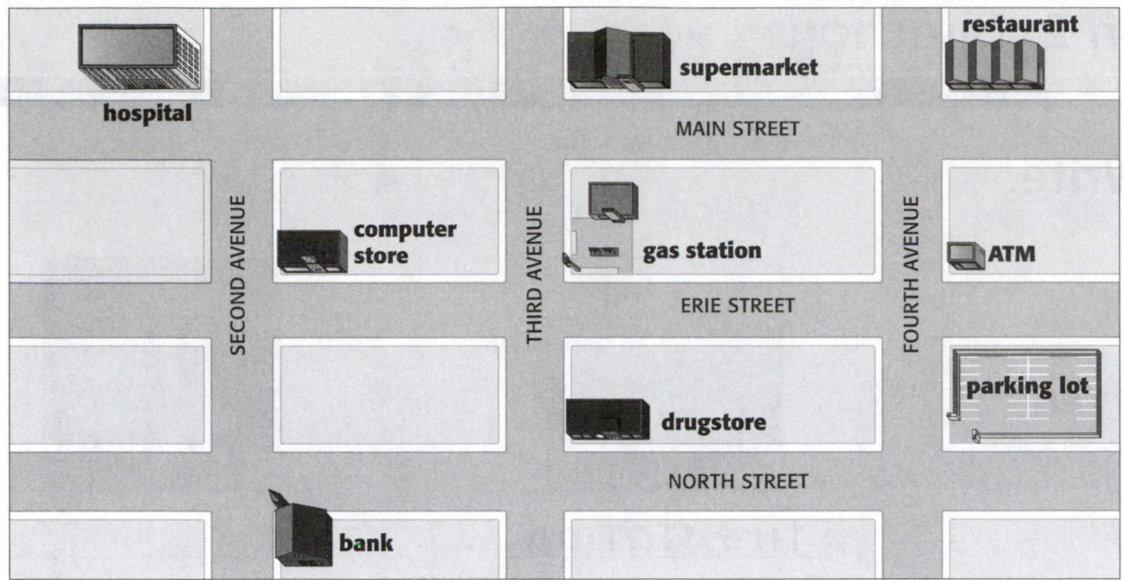

C Write.

bank	~~drugstore~~	hospital
restaurant	supermarket	

1. There's a ___drugstore___ on the corner of North Street and Third Avenue.
2. There's a ________________ on the corner of North Street and Second Avenue.
3. There's a ________________ on the corner of Main Street and Second Avenue.
4. There's a ________________ on the corner of Main Street and Third Avenue.
5. There's a ________________ on the corner of Main Street and Fourth Avenue.

A Write.

courthouse
fire station

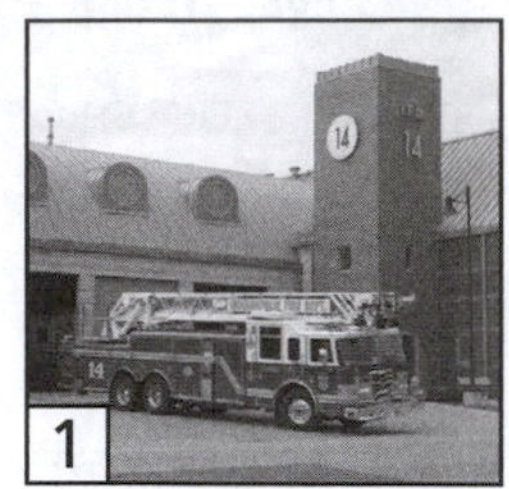

1

fire station

2

library
park

3

4

police station
post office

5

6

school
City Hall

7

8

B T76 Listen. Check your answers.

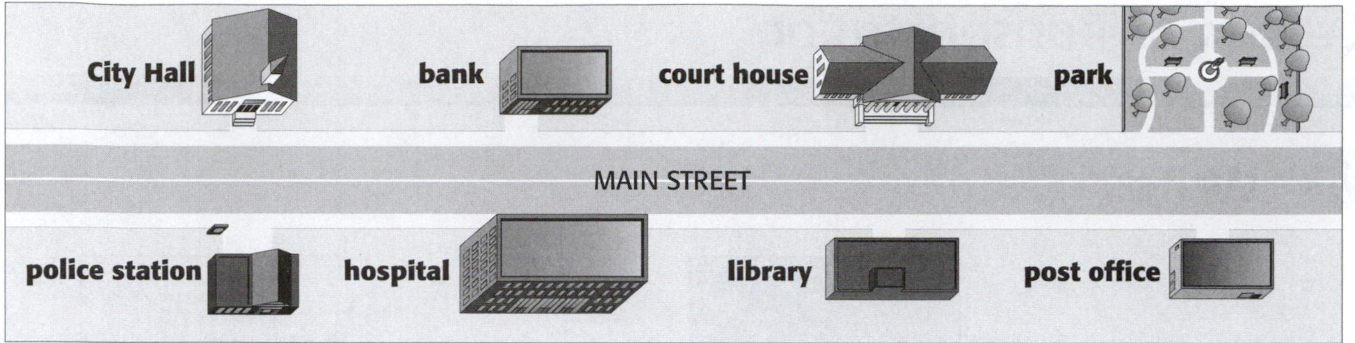

Ⓒ Look. Write.

1. Where is City Hall?

   It's across from the ________________.

2. Where is the courthouse?

   It's between the bank and the ________________.

3. Where is the park?

   It's across from the ________________.

4. Where is the hospital?

   It's between the police station and the ________________.

5. Where is the hospital?

   It's across from the ________________.

6. Where is the library?

   It's between the post office and the ________________.

A Write.

bus
subway

take the subway

take the ______

train
taxi

take a ______

take the ______

drive
walk

______

6

______

carpool
ride

______

8

______ a bike

B T77 Listen. Check your answers.

C Read. Underline the transportation words.

My name is Alice. My husband and I don't drive. I take a taxi to the supermarket. My daughter takes the bus to school. My husband takes the subway to work.

D Read again. Write.

1. How does Alice get to the supermarket?

   She takes a taxi to the supermarket.

2. How does her daughter get to school?

   ____

3. How does her husband get to work?

   ____

E Write about you.

1. How do you get to school?

   ____

2. How do you get to the supermarket?

   ____

Lesson 4: Directions

A Match.

1. 

2. 

3. 

turn right

go straight

turn left

B T78 Listen and circle.

1. Go straight. Turn left. Turn right.
2. Go straight. Turn left. Turn right.
3. Go straight. Turn left. Turn right.
4. Go straight. Turn left. Turn right.

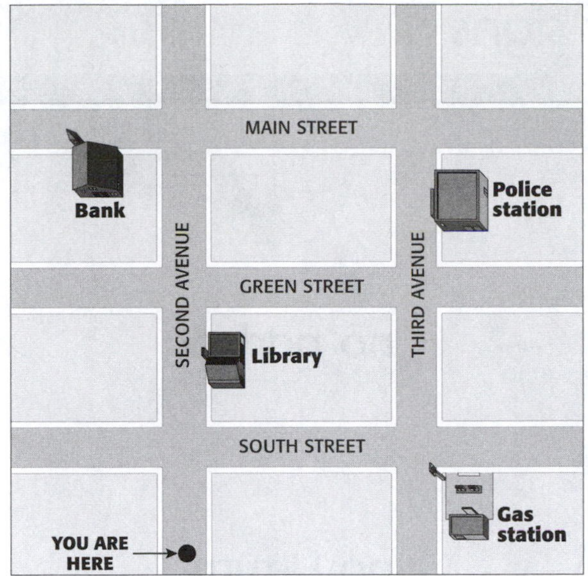

C Look. Write.

straight	left	right

1. Directions to the library.

   Go ___straight___ one block.

2. Directions to the gas station.

   Turn ______________ on South Street.

   Go ______________ one block.

3. Directions to the police station.

   Go ______________ two blocks.

   Turn ______________ on Green Street.

   Turn ______________ on Third Avenue.

4. Directions to the bank.

   Go ______________ three blocks.

   Turn ______________ on Main Street.

Lesson 5: Traffic signs

A Match.

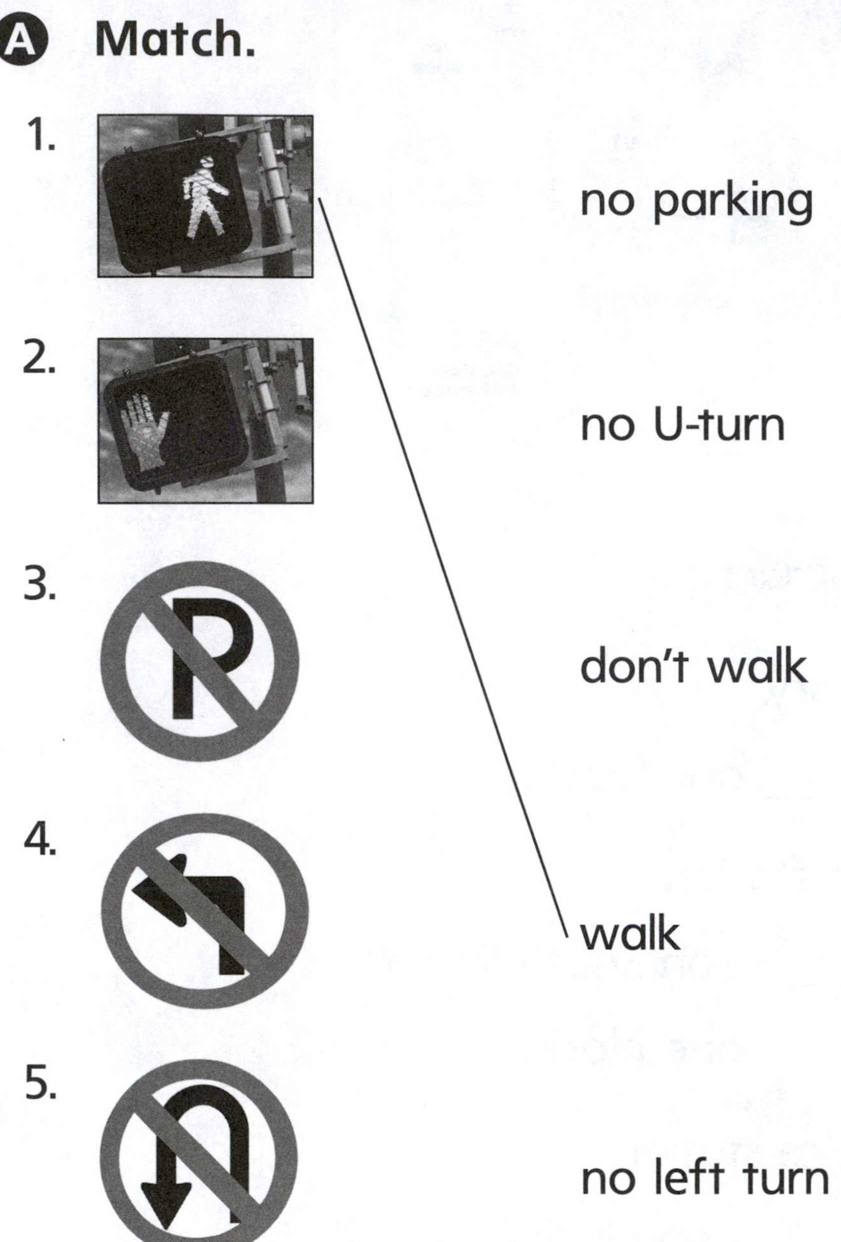

1. no parking
2. no U-turn
3. don't walk
4. walk
5. no left turn

B T79 Listen. Check your answers.

C T80 Listen and circle.

1.

2.

3.

4.

5.

D What signs do you see in your school?

Copy one school sign in your notebook.

____

E What signs do you see on the street?

Copy one street sign in your notebook.

____

A Listen and write.

T81

bank	business	City Hall
~~cook~~	dream	restaurant

1. My name is Hong. I'm a ______cook______.
2. I have a ____________________.
3. I want to open my own ____________________.
4. I need to get a restaurant license at ____________________.
5. I need to get a loan at the ____________________.
6. Now I can open my own ____________________.

B Write about you.

I have a dream. I want to ______________________________

____

____

Phonics

A T82 **Listen and write.** **Copy.**

a i

1. <u>a</u>nd ______
2. b__ke ______
3. b__nk ______
4. dr__ve ______
5. f__ve ______
6. g__s ______
7. r__de ______
8. th__nks ______

B T83 **Listen and write.** **Copy.**

r w

1. <u>w</u>alk ______
2. __ead ______
3. __atch ______
4. __estaurant ______
5. __ork ______
6. __ight ______

Unit 11: Get well soon!

Lesson 1: The body

A   T84 **Listen and point.**

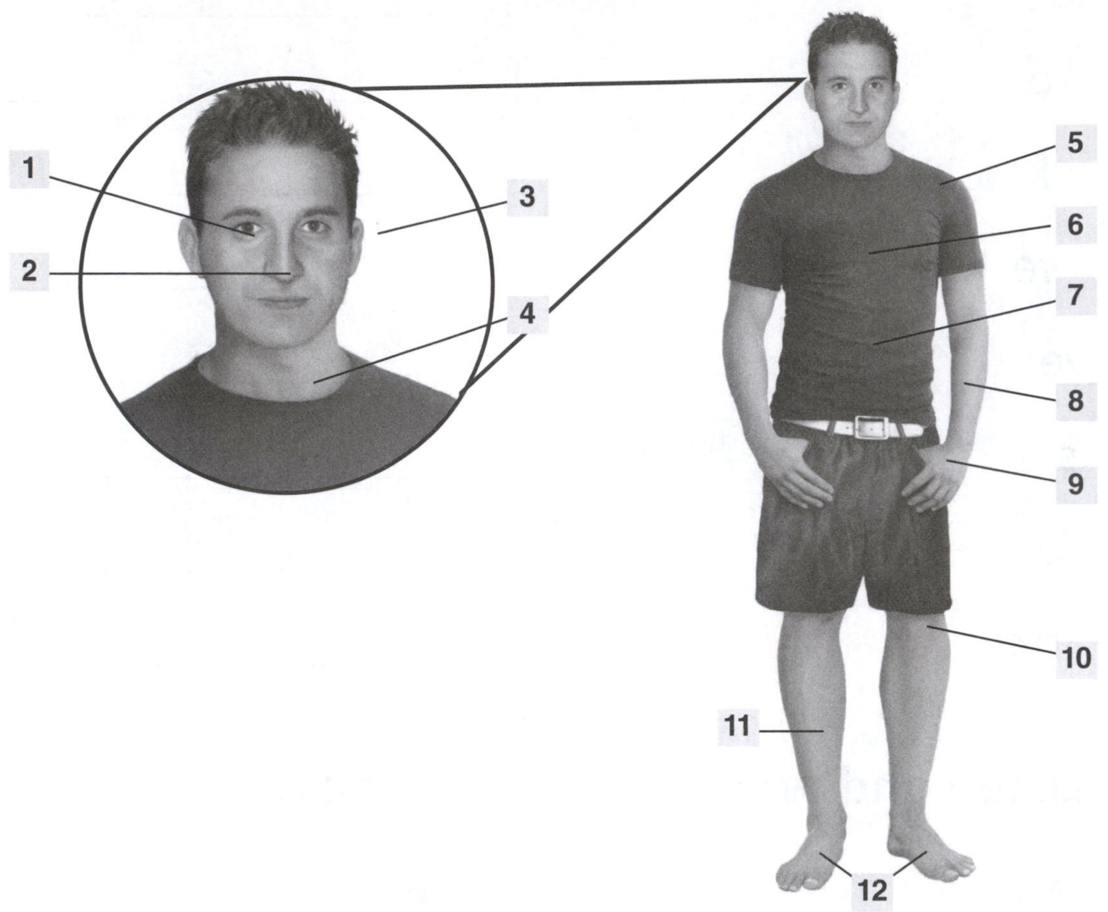

B **Trace.**

1.	eye	5.	shoulder	9.	hand
2.	nose	6.	chest	10.	knee
3.	ear	7.	stomach	11.	leg
4.	neck	8.	arm	12.	feet

C Circle the same.

1. **eye**	eyes	ear	(eye)
2. **stomach**	shoulder	stomachache	stomach
3. **foot**	feet	foot	finger
4. **nose**	no	neck	nose
5. **hand**	hands	hand	handle

D Write.

hand	neck	shoulder	stomach

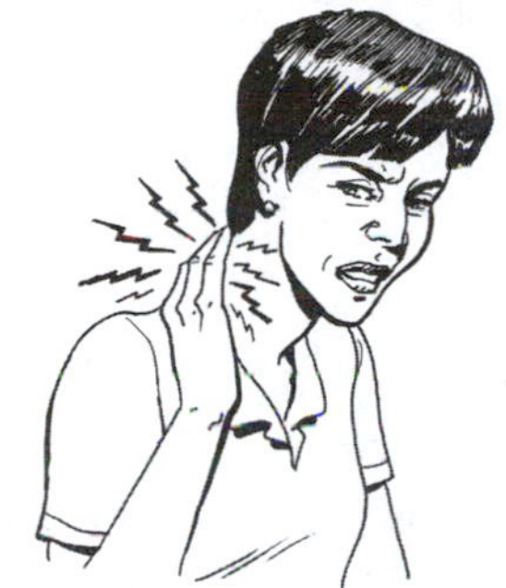

1. Her __________ hurts.

2. His __________ hurts.

3. Her __________ hurts.

4. His __________ hurts.

Lesson 2: At the doctor's office

A Match.

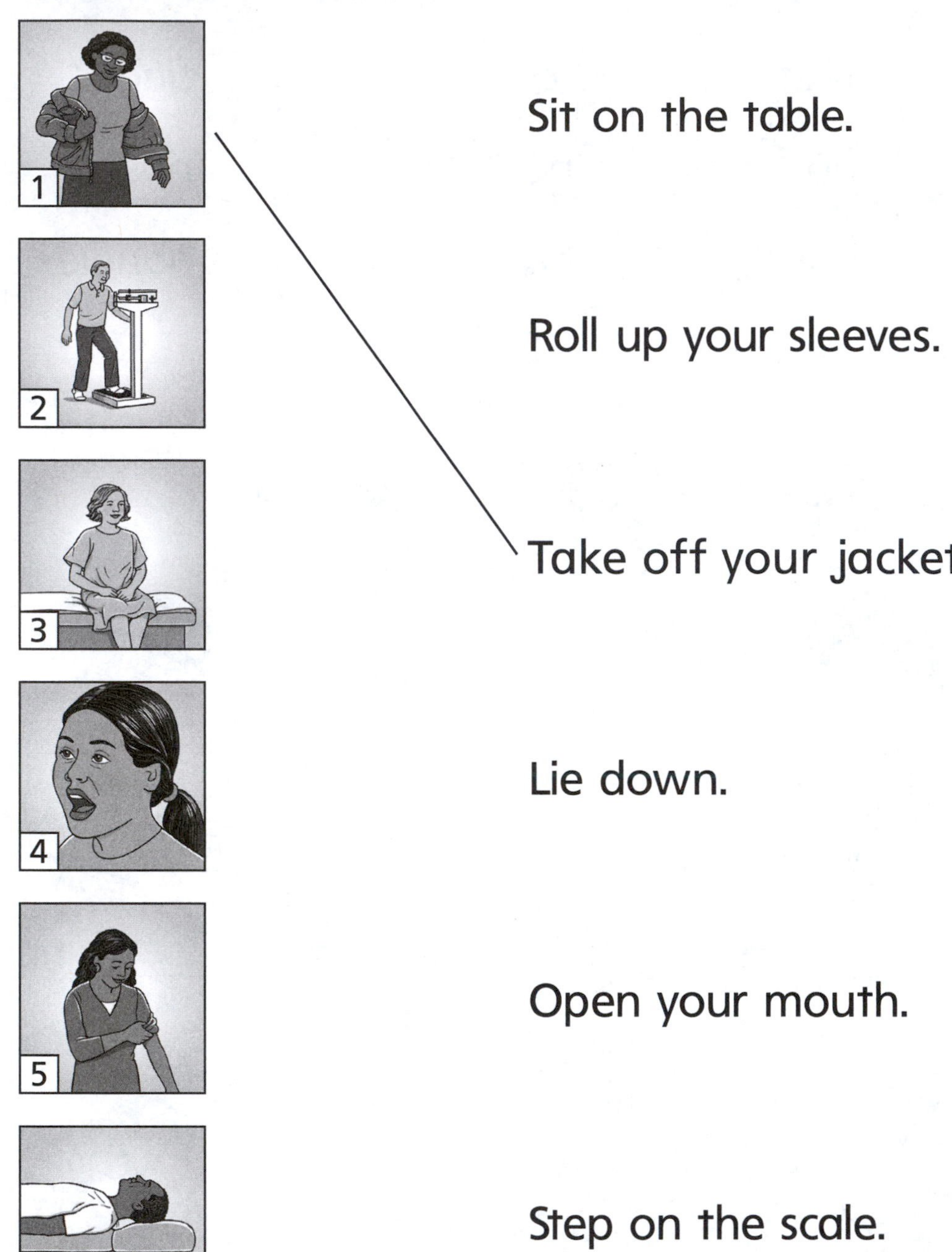

1
2
3
4
5
6
Sit on the table.
Roll up your sleeves.
Take off your jacket.
Lie down.
Open your mouth.
Step on the scale.

B T85 **Listen. Check your answers.**

C T86 Listen and circle.

1.	Lie down on the table.	Sit down.
2.	Open your eyes.	Open your mouth.
3.	Step on the scale.	Step off the scale.
4.	Roll up your pants.	Roll up your sleeves.
5.	Sit on the table.	Sit on the chair.
6.	Take off your jacket.	Take off your shoes.

D Write.

Lie	Open	Roll up	~~Sit~~	Step	Take off

1. ____Sit____ on the table.
2. ________ your shoes.
3. ________ down.
4. ________ your mouth.
5. ________ your sleeves.
6. ________ on the scale.

Lesson 3: Health problems

A T87 **Listen and point.**

B **Trace. Copy.**

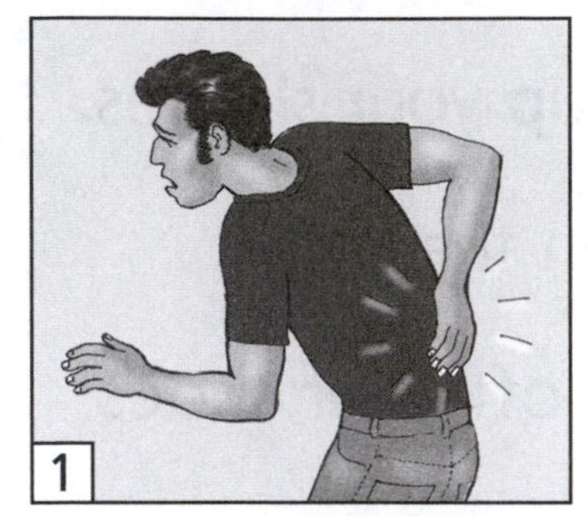
1

a backache

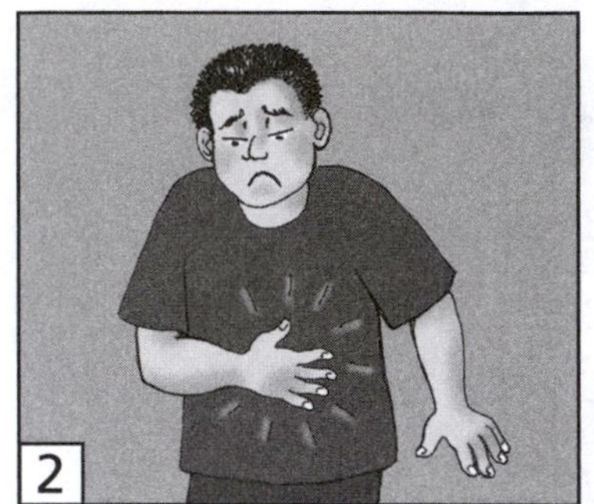
2

a stomachache

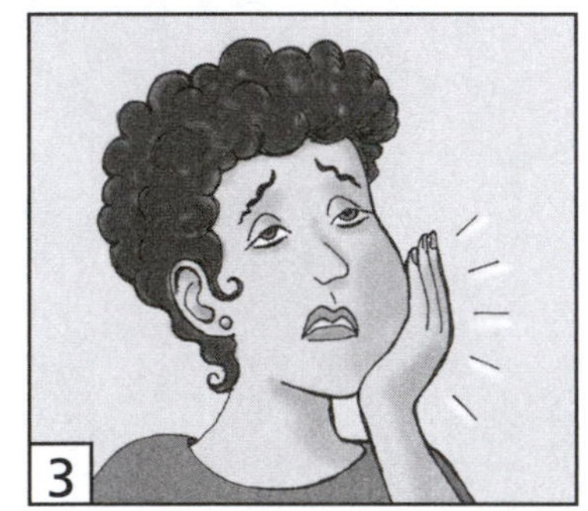
3

a toothache

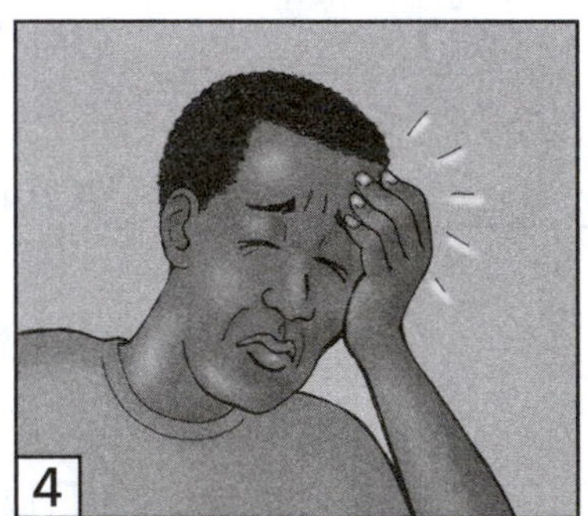
4

a headache

C **Underline the same.**

ache head<u>ache</u> backache stomachache toothache

D Write.

a cough
a sore throat

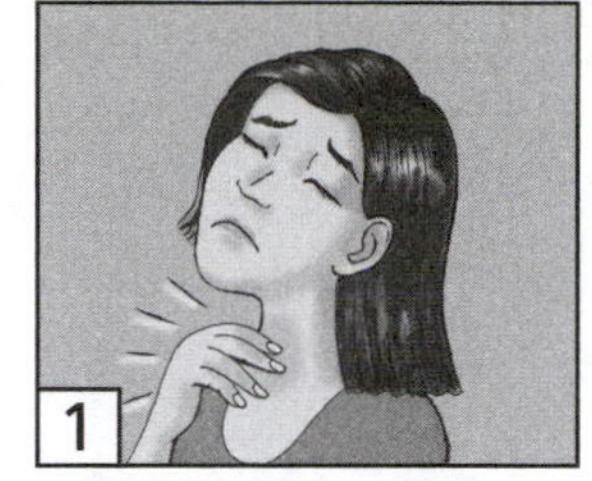
1

____

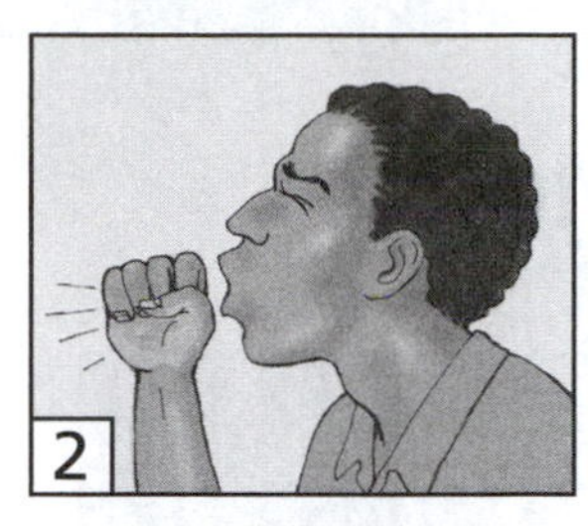
2

____

a cold
a fever

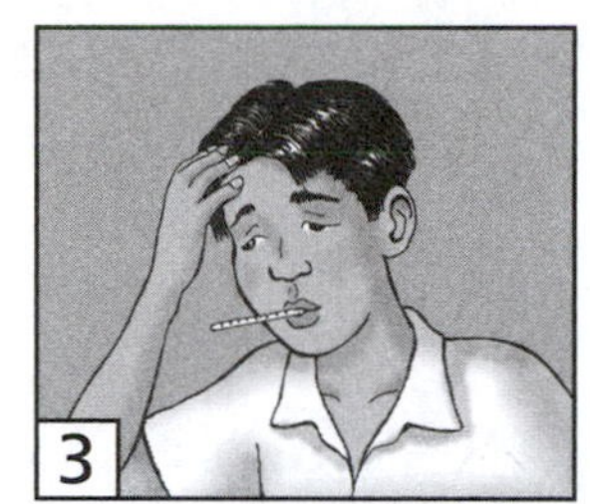
3

____

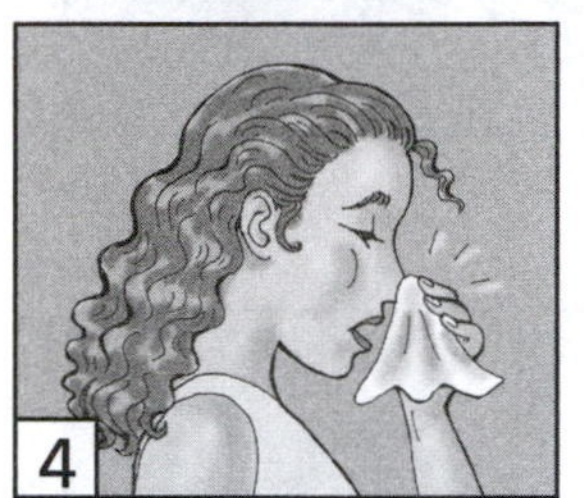
4

____

E T88 Listen. Check your answers.

F Read. Circle *Yes* or *No*.

Elsa is sick. She has a sore throat and a fever. Elsa is not going to school today. She needs to stay home.

1. Elsa is sick. Yes No
2. Elsa has a fever. (Yes) No
3. Elsa has a headache. Yes No
4. Elsa is going to school today. Yes No

Lesson 4: Call 911

A Match.

There is a fire.

My house was robbed.

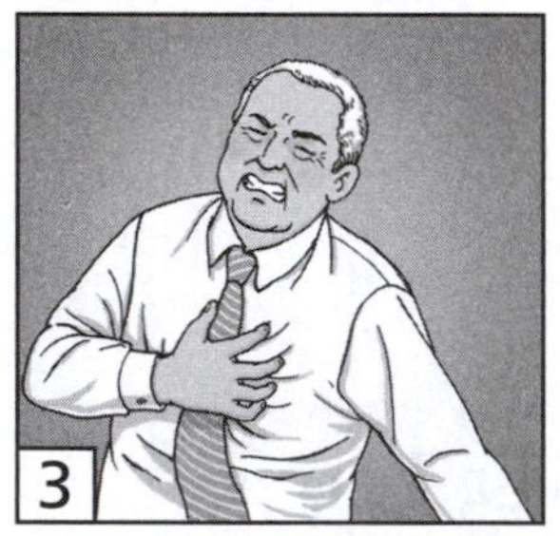

There was a car accident.

A man is having a heart attack.

B  Listen. Check your answers.

C Match.

1. What's your emergency? —— My house was robbed.
2. Where are you? —— 112 Main Street.

3. What's your emergency? —— 55 Lake Boulevard.
4. Where are you? —— There was a car accident.

5. What's your emegency? —— 19 Bankers Street.
6. Where are you? —— A woman is having a heart attack.

D Write.

~~emergency~~	fire	Street	Where

A: 911. What's your __emergency__?

B: There is a ________________.

A: ________________ are you?

B: 374 Green ________________.

Lesson 5: Medicine

A **Match.**

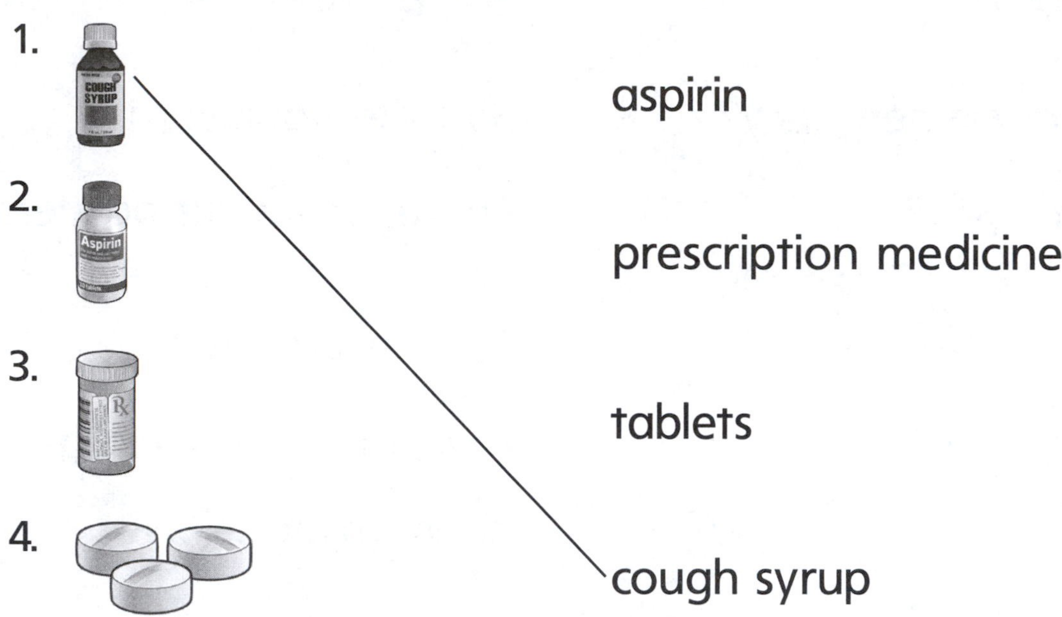

1.
2.
3.
4.

aspirin

prescription medicine

tablets

cough syrup

B T90 **Listen. Check your answers.**

C **Read. Write the number.**

4	6	12

1. I take the medicine at 12:00 and 6:00.
   I take the medicine every ____ hours.
2. I take the medicine at 2:00 P.M., 6:00 P.M., and 10:00 P.M.
   I take the medicine every ____ hours.
3. I take the medicine at 11:00 in the morning and night.
   I take the medicine every ____ hours.

D Read. Circle *Yes* or *No*.

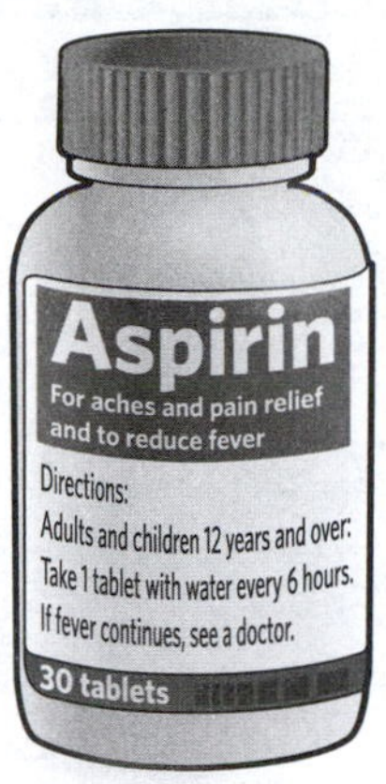

1.	The medicine is aspirin.	(Yes)	No
2.	Take 1 tablet every 4 hours.	Yes	No
3.	The medicine is for pain and fever.	Yes	No
4.	It is prescription medicine.	Yes	No
5.	The medicine is for children under 12.	Yes	No
6.	There are 60 tablets.	Yes	No

E Circle *Yes* or *No* about you.

Sometimes I take prescription medicine.	Yes	No
Sometimes I take aspirin.	Yes	No
Sometimes I take cough syrup.	Yes	No

F Copy your *Yes* sentences in your notebook.

A T91 **Listen and write.**

doctor	checkup	feel	Healthy
~~name~~	sick	stay	

1. My ____name____ is Mariam.
2. In my country, __________ people go to the doctor.
3. In the U.S., everyone goes to the __________.
4. __________ people have a checkup every year.
5. I don't feel sick. I __________ healthy.
6. Why do I need a __________?
7. I need a checkup to __________ healthy.

B **Circle *Yes* or *No* about you.**

I go to the doctor when I am sick.	Yes	No
I go to the doctor for checkups.	Yes	No

A T92 **Listen and write.** **Copy.**

ee e

1. n_ee_d ______
2. n__ck ______
3. f____t ______
4. l__g ______
5. str____t ______
6. st__p ______
7. kn____ ______
8. ch__ckup ______

B T93 **Listen and write.** **Copy.**

a i

1. s_i_t ______
2. t__blets ______
3. h__s ______
4. b__g ______
5. s__ck ______
6. b__ck ______

Unit 12: What do you do?

Lesson 1: Jobs

 **Write.**

construction worker
painter

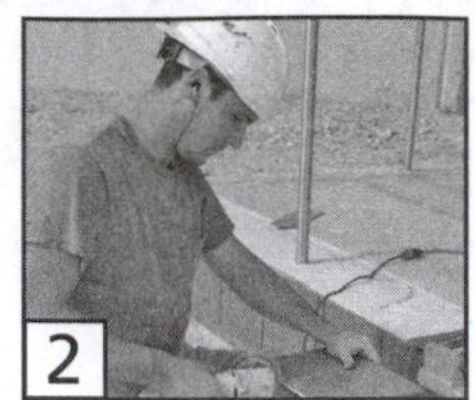

mechanic
homemaker

housekeeper
teacher's assistant

bus driver
sales assistant

  T94 **Listen. Check your answers.**

C Underline *er*. Cover and write.

1. a homemaker ______________________
2. a driver ______________________
3. a housekeeper ______________________
4. a painter ______________________
5. a worker ______________________

D What do you do? Write.

a construction worker	a dentist
~~a mechanic~~	a sales assistant

I'm *a mechanic*.

I'm ______________________.

I'm ______________________.

I'm ______________________.

E What do you do? Write about you.

I'm a ______________________.

Lesson 2: More jobs

A Write.

custodian
security guard

1 security guard

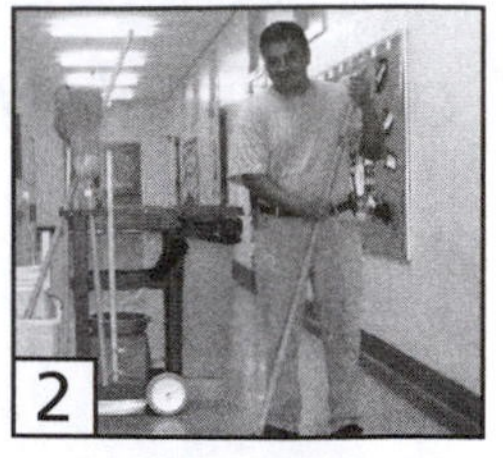

2 ______________

cashier
office assistant

3 ______________

4 ______________

cook
factory worker

5 ______________

6 ______________

nurse
waiter

7 ______________

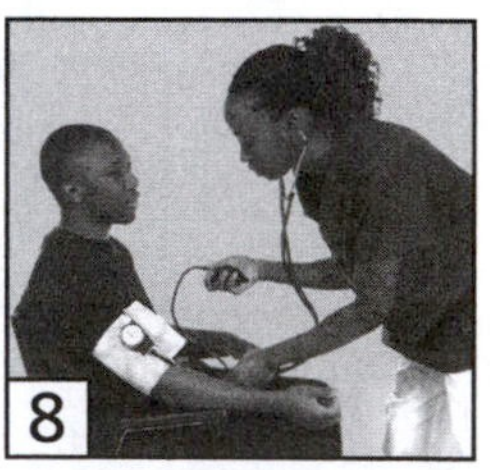

8 ______________

B T95 Listen. Check your answers.

C Match.

1. What do you do? — I'm a cashier.
2. What does he do?
3. Where does she work?
4. What do they do?
5. Where do they work?

They're custodians.

He's a waiter.

I'm a cashier.

They work in a hospital.

She works in a store.

D Write.

cook security guard
factory worker nurse
bus driver cashier
dentist sales assistant
housekeeper teacher's assistant
office assistant waiter

1. He works in a bank.
   He's a *security guard*.
2. She works in a hospital.
   She's a ________________.
3. She works in a supermarket.
   She's a ________________.
4. He works in a store.
   He's a ________________.
5. She works in a school.
   She's a ________________.
6. He works in an office.
   He's an ________________.

Lesson 3: Job skills

A Write.

drive
use

1

drive a truck

2

_______ a computer

help
use

3

_______ customers

4

_______ a cash register

speak
fix

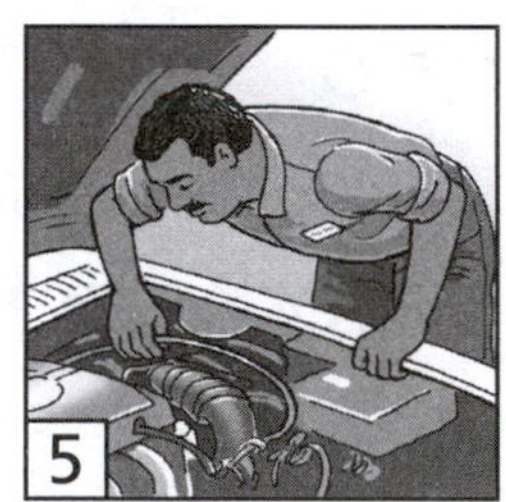
5

_______ cars

6

_______ two languages

use
build

7

_______ homes

8

_______ office machines

B  T96 Listen. Check your answers.

C Match.

1.	cashier	I help sick people.
2.	sales assistant	I fix cars.
3.	office assistant	I help customers.
4.	construction worker	I use a cash register.
5.	mechanic	I use office machines.
6.	nurse	I build houses.

D Circle *Yes* or *No* about you.

I speak two languages.	Yes	No
I build houses.	Yes	No
I fix cars.	Yes	No
I fix houses.	Yes	No
I cook.	Yes	No
I help sick people.	Yes	No

E Copy your *Yes* sentences in your notebook.

Ms. Rami talks about her job skills.

A Read.

Mr. Jones:	What are your job skills?
Ms. Rami:	I use a computer.
Mr. Jones:	Can you use a cash register?
Ms. Rami:	No, I can't.
Mr. Jones:	Can you help customers?
Ms. Rami:	Yes, I can.
Mr. Jones:	Can you speak two languages?
Ms. Rami:	No, I can't.

B Circle *Yes* or *No*.

1. Ms. Rami can use a computer. Yes No
2. She can use a cash register. Yes No
3. Ms. Rami can help customers. Yes No
4. She can speak two languages. Yes No

C Write about you.

	Yes, I can.	No, I can't.
1. Can you use a computer?		
2. Can you fix cars?		
3. Can you speak two languages?		
4. Can you drive a car?		
5. Can you drive a truck?		
6. Can you use a cash register?		
7. Can you build houses?		
8. Can you speak English?		

D Write your job skills.

1. I can ______________________________
2. I can ______________________________
3. I can ______________________________

Lesson 5: Read a job ad

A Match.

1. week days — 15 hours a week
2. weekends — 40 hours a week
3. part-time — Saturdays and Sundays
4. full-time — Monday to Friday

B Read. Circle *Yes* or *No*.

Cashier
Full-time
Monday to Friday
City Supermarket
Call 459-555-1249

1. The job is for a cashier. Yes No
2. The job is on weekdays. Yes No
3. The job is part-time. Yes No
4. The job is in a supermarket. Yes No

C Match.

1.	weekends	M-F
2.	part-time	FT
3.	week days	wknds
4.	full-time	hrs/wk
5.	hours a week	PT

D Read. Circle *Yes* and *No*.

Custodian
PT 25 hrs/wk
wknds
City Hospital
Call 718-555-3247

1.	The job is for a housekeeper.	Yes	No
2.	The job is full-time.	Yes	No
3.	The job is 30 hours a week.	Yes	No
4.	The job is in a hospital.	Yes	No
5.	The job is on Saturdays and Sundays.	Yes	No

Lesson 6: Monika's story

A T97 **Listen and write.**

early	eye contact	job	~~name~~	shake hands

1. My ___name___ is Monika.
2. I have a ______________ interview on Thursday.
3. I need to get there ______________.
4. I need to ______________ with the interviewer.
5. I need to make ______________ when we talk.

B **Circle *Yes* or *No*.**

1. Monika has a job interview on Tuesday. Yes No
2. Monika needs to get to the interview early. Yes No
3. Monika needs to shake hands with the interviewer. Yes No
4. Monika needs to look at the interviewer when they talk. Yes No

Phonics

  T98

Listen and write.

Copy.

o u

1. j o b ____________
2. __p ____________
3. b__s ____________
4. st__p ____________
5. tr__ck ____________
6. sh__p ____________

B T99 Listen and circle.

1.	paint	painter
2.	wait	waiter
3.	teach	teacher
4.	work	worker
5.	drive	driver
6.	write	writer
7.	interview	interviewer
8.	call	caller

Audio Script

UNIT 1

Page 3, Exercise C

A: Hi. My name is Chen.
B: Hello. I'm Pam.

Page 3, Exercise D

A: Where are you from?
B: I'm from the U.S.

Page 5, Exercise B

1. 754 - 555 - 3921
2. 935 - 555 - 6298
3. 443 - 555 - 4536
4. 915 - 555 - 7187

Page 8, Exercise C

1. She's a teacher.
2. He's a student.
3. He's a friend.
4. She's from the U.S.
5. He's my classmate.

Page 10, Exercise C

1. They're students.
2. We're friends.
3. They're classmates.
4. You're my friend.
5. We're from the U.S.
6. You're a teacher.

Page 12, Exercise B

1. Students say hello and shake hands.
2. Students say hello and hug.
3. Students say hello and bow.
4. Students say hello and kiss.

Page 13, Exercise A

1. name
2. number
3. my
4. middle name
5. new
6. meet

Page 13, Exercise B

1. hello
2. friend
3. first name
4. hi
5. from
6. hug

UNIT 2

Page 16, Exercise B

1. Turn on the light.
2. Turn off the light.
3. Open your book.
4. Close your dictionary.
5. Take out your pencil.
6. Put away your book.

Page 17, Exercise C

1. Close the door.
2. Turn on the light.
3. Put away your pencil.
4. Don't open your book.
5. Take out your pen.
6. Don't turn off the light.

Page 19, Exercise D

1. classroom
2. bookstore
3. classmate
4. cell phone
5. notebook
6. men's room
7. telephone
8. women's room

Page 23, Exercise B

1. I go to class.
2. I practice English with my classmates.
3. I ask the teacher questions.
4. I use a dictionary.
5. I write in my notebook.
6. I read signs.

Page 24, Exercise B

1. Students don't talk in class.
2. Students listen to the teacher.
3. Students talk in groups.
4. Students ask questions.

Page 25, Exercise A

1. pen
2. paper
3. book
4. backpack
5. pencil
6. put away

Page 25, Exercise B

1. notebook
2. men
3. male
4. next to
5. my

UNIT 3

Page 30, Exercise B

1. get up
2. go to sleep
3. take a shower
4. get dressed
5. eat breakfast
6. eat lunch
7. go to work
8. go to school

Page 33, Exercise C

1. Sunday
2. Monday
3. Tuesday
4. Wednesday
5. Thursday
6. Friday
7. Saturday

Page 34, Exercise B

1. 70
2. 100
3. 60
4. 90
5. 80

Page 35, Exercise C

1. 20
2. 13
3. 14
4. 50
5. 60
6. 17
7. 80
8. 19

Page 35, Exercise D

1. 2:00
2. 2:30
3. 2:15
4. 2:50
5. 2:20
6: 2:40

Page 36, Exercise A

1. Carlo likes to be on time.
2. He gets up early and gets ready for work.
3. He arrives at 6:50, and starts work at 7:00.
4. Carlo goes to school after work.
5. He is always early for class.
6. But Carlo is always late meeting friends!

Page 37, Exercise A

1. dinner
2. to
3. teacher
4. day
5. time
6. do

Page 37, Exercise B

1. Saturday
2. Monday
3. Thursday
4. Wednesday
5. Friday
6. Sunday
7. Tuesday

UNIT 4

Page 39, Exercise D

1. sister
2. mother
3. grandfather
4. daughter
5. children
6. husband

Page 42, Exercise B

1. vacuum
2. do the laundry
3. take out the garbage
4. wash the dishes
5. make dinner
6. clean the house

Page 45, Exercise C

1. January
2. March
3. December
4. July
5. August
6. September

Page 48, Exercise A

1. Ernesto and Maria are married.
2. In their country, men go to work.
3. Women stay at home.
4. In their country, women do all the household chores.
5. In the United States, they both go to work.
6. Ernesto helps at home.
7. He does the dishes.
8. He goes to the supermarket.

Page 49, Exercise A

1. middle
2. birth
3. date
4. place
5. mother
6. name
7. daughter
8. parents

Page 49, Exercise B

1. March
2. May
3. November
4. December

UNIT 5

Page 50, Exercise B

1. a penny
2. a nickel
3. a dime
4. a quarter
5. a dollar

Page 52, Exercise B

1. One dollar
2. Five dollars
3. Ten dollars
4. Twenty dollars
5. Fifty dollars
6. One hundred dollars

Page 54, Exercise B

1. batteries
2. soap
3. toilet paper
4. lightbulbs
5. toothpaste
6. tissues
7. paper towels
8. razor blades

Page 57, Exercise B

1. $ 1.59
2. $86.49
3. $ 7.28
4. $59.63
5. $95.40
6. $32.15

Page 60, Exercise A

1. My name is Edna.
2. I shop at markets.
3. I talk about the prices.
4. I get good bargains.
5. I shop in big stores.
6. I pay the price on the price tag.
7. I buy things on sale.

Page 61, Exercise A

1. coin
2. go
3. get
4. good
5. country
6. cost

Page 61, Exercise B

1. dime
2. bargain
3. buy
4. dollar
5. batteries
6. date

UNIT 6

Page 64, Exercise A

1. onions
2. tomatoes
3. lettuce
4. peppers
5. carrots
6. peas
7. mushrooms
8. potatoes

Page 64, Exercise B

1. I like vegetables.
2. We don't like mushrooms.
3. They like tomatoes.
4. I don't like onions.
5. They don't like carrots.
6. We like peas.

Page 66, Exercise B

1. peaches
2. bananas
3. oranges
4. pears
5. strawberries
6. cherries
7. grapes
8. apples

Page 68, Exercise B

1. milk
2. bread
3. eggs
4. cereal
5. chicken
6. fish
7. soup
8. rice

Page 72, Exercise B

1. Some people eat with chopsticks.
2. Some people eat with their fingers.
3. Some people drink their soup.
4. Some people eat with forks, knives, and spoons.

Page 73, Exercise A

1. soup
2. fish
3. vegetable
4. food
5. fruit
6. salad
7. fingers

Page 73, Exercise B

1. carrots
2. chicken
3. cucumbers
4. cherries
5. lunch
6. sandwich

UNIT 7

Page 74, Exercise B

1. bedroom
2. kitchen
3. living room
4. bathroom
5. dining room
6. laundry room

Page 80, Exercise A

1. 13
2. 40
3. 5
4. 16
5. 70
6. 18

Page 80, Exercise B

1. 30 River Drive
2. 88 Lake Boulevard
3. 60 Park Avenue
4. 14 Bank Street
5. 75 North Road
6. 19 City Lane

Page 81, Exercise C

1. seven fifty-five
2. two seventy
3. eight thirty-six
4. twenty-four
5. three thirty

Page 84, Exercise A

1. Alicia is 21 years old.
2. She is single.
3. She lives with her sister and her brother-in-law.
4. Alicia has a good job.
5. She wants to live with her friends.
6. Her parents are not happy.
7. In their country, single people live with family.

Page 85, Exercise A

1. lamp
2. room
3. living room
4. rent
5. road
6. laundry

Page 85, Exercise B

1. bed
2. dining room
3. bathroom
4. boulevard
5. drive
6. dresser

UNIT 8

Page 90, Exercise A

1. blue
2. pink
3. gray
4. beige
5. purple
6. brown
7. green
8. black

Page 96, Exercise A

1. My name is Yun. In my country, women wear red and green on their wedding day.
2. People wear white for funerals.
3. I want to wear a white dress for my wedding.
4. My mother wants me to wear a red and green dress on my wedding day.

Page 97, Exercise A

1. short
2. sale
3. shirt
4. size
5. socks
6. shoes
7. suit
8. shopping

Page 97, Exercise B

1. gray
2. jeans
3. jacket
4. green

UNIT 9

Page 98, Exercise B

1. play the guitar
2. read the newspaper
3. watch TV
4. listen to music
5. go to the movies
6. exercise
7. visit friends
8. play soccer

Page 100, Exercise A

1. You're playing the guitar.
2. She's watching a movie.
3. I'm exercising.
4. He's reading the newspaper.
5. We're listening to music.
6. They're going to the movies.

Page 102, Exercise B

1. doing homework
2. talking on the phone
3. making dinner
4. taking out the garbage
5. paying bills
6. doing the laundry
7. washing the car
8. walking the dog

Page 104, Exercise B

1. He's looking for something.
2. He's helping a customer.
3. She's taking a break.
4. He's fixing cars.
5. He's taking orders.

Page 107, Exercise C

1. A: Can I take a message?
   B: Please tell him I'm not coming to work today.
2. A: Can I take a message?
   B: Please tell her I'm driving to work today.
3. A: Can I take a message?
   B: Please tell her my children are coming to school late today.

Page 107, Exercise D

A: Can I take a message?
B: Please tell him I'm not driving to work today.

Page 107, Exercise E

A: Can I take a message?
B: Please tell her I'm coming to work late today.

Page 108, Exercise A

1. My name is Alfonso.
2. Every weekend, my children are busy with their friends.
3. They talk on the phone with their friends.
4. They go shopping with their friends.
5. They play sports with their friends.
6. In my country, children spend time with their family on the weekends.
7. They eat dinner with their family.
8. They sit and talk with their family.

Page 109, Exercise A

1. play
2. pay
3. day
4. away

Page 109, Exercise B

1. yes
2. hello
3. yellow
4. help

Page 109, Exercise C

1. take	make	talk
2. late	last	date
3. red	read	bed
4. ten	pen	tea

UNIT 10

Page 110, Exercise B

1. a hospital
2. a bank
3. a gas station
4. a parking lot
5. a restaurant
6. a supermarket
7. a drugstore
8. an ATM

Page 112, Exercise B

1. fire station
2. courthouse
3. park
4. library
5. post office
6. police station
7. school
8. City Hall

Page 114, Exercise B

1. take the subway
2. take the bus
3. take a taxi
4. take the train
5. walk
6. drive
7. carpool
8. ride a bike

Page 116, Exercise B

1. Go straight two blocks.
2. Turn left on Main Street.
3. Go straight one block.
4. Turn right on First Avenue.

Page 118, Exercise B

1. walk
2. don't walk
3. no parking
4. no left turn
5. no U-turn

Page 119, Exercise C

1. train crossing
2. yield
3. speed limit
4. one-way street
5. stop

Page 120, Exercise A

1. My name is Hong. I'm a cook.
2. I have a dream.
3. I want to open my own restaurant.
4. I need to get a restaurant license at City Hall.
5. I need to get a loan at the bank.
6. Now I can open my own business.

Page 121, Exercise A

1. and
2. bike
3. bank
4. drive
5. five
6. gas
7. ride
8. thanks

Page 121, Exercise B

1. walk
2. read
3. watch
4. restaurant
5. work
6. right

UNIT 11

Page 124, Exercise B

1. Take off your jacket.
2. Step on the scale.
3. Sit on the table.
4. Open your mouth.
5. Roll up your sleeves.
6. Lie down.

Page 125, Exercise C

1. Lie down on the table.
2. Open your mouth.
3. Step on the scale.
4. Roll up your pants.
5. Sit on the table.
6. Take off your shoes.

Page 127, Exercise E

1. a sore throat
2. a cough
3. a fever
4. a cold

Page 128, Exercise B

1. My house was robbed.
2. There was a car accident.
3. A man is having a heart attack.
4. There is a fire.

Page 130, Exercise B

1. cough syrup
2. aspirin
3. prescription medicine
4. tablets

Page 132, Exercise A

1. My name is Mariam.
2. In my country, sick people go to the doctor.
3. In the U.S., everyone goes to the doctor.
4. Healthy people have a checkup every year.
5. I don't feel sick. I feel healthy.
6. Why do I need a checkup?
7. I need a checkup to stay healthy.

Page 133, Exercise A

1. need
2. neck
3. feet
4. leg
5. street
6. step
7. knee
8. checkup

Page 133, Exercise B

1. sit
2. tablets
3. his
4. big
5. sick
6. back

UNIT 12

Page 134, Exercise B

1. painter
2. construction worker
3. mechanic
4. homemaker
5. teacher's assistant
6. housekeeper
7. bus driver
8. sales assistant

Page 136, Exercise B

1. security guard
2. custodian
3. office assistant
4. cashier
5. cook
6. factory worker
7. waiter
8. nurse

Page 138, Exercise B

1. drive a truck
2. use a computer
3. help customers
4. use a cash register
5. fix cars
6. speak two languages
7. build homes
8. use office machines

Page 144, Exercise A

1. My name is Monika.
2. I have a job interview on Thursday.
3. I need to get there early.
4. I need to shake hands with the interviewer.
5. I need to make eye contact when we talk.

Page 145, Exercise A

1. job
2. up
3. bus
4. stop
5. truck
6. shop

Page 145, Exercise B

1. painter
2. wait
3. teacher
4. work
5. driver
6. write
7. interview
8. caller